YOU CAN DRAW
COMIC BOOK
CHaRaCTeRS

A step-by-step guide for
learning to draw more than
25 comic book characters

WRITTEN & ILLUSTRATED BY SPENCER BRINKERHOFF III

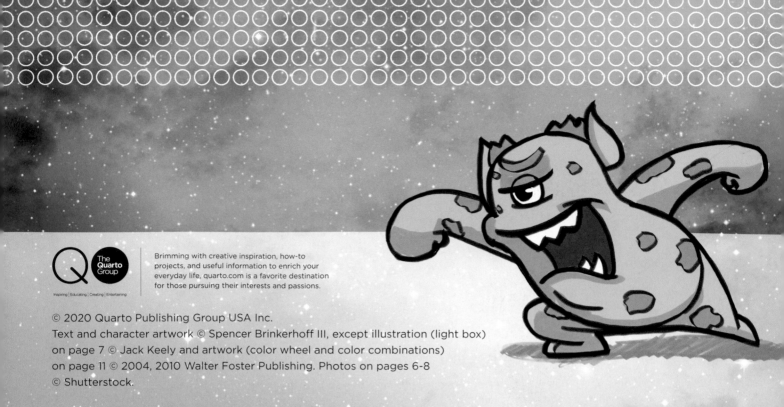

First published in 2020 by Walter Foster Jr., an imprint of The Quarto Group.
100 Cummings Center, Suite 265D, Beverly, MA 01915, USA.
T (978) 282-9590 **F** (978) 283-2742 **www.quarto.com** • **www.walterfoster.com**

Walter Foster Jr. titles are also available at discount for retail, wholesale, promotional, and bulk purchase. For details, contact the Special Sales Manager by email at specialsales@quarto.com or by mail at The Quarto Group, Attn: Special Sales Manager, 100 Cummings Center, Suite 265D, Beverly, MA 01915, USA.

ISBN: 978-1-63322-866-5

Digital edition published in 2020
eISBN: 978-1-63322-867-2

Printed in Canada
10 9 8 7 6 5 4 3 2

MIX
Paper from
responsible sources
FSC
www.fsc.org FSC® C011825

Contents

ZAP!

POW!

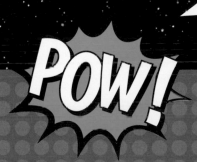

Introduction

Hi, comic book fans!

My name is Spencer, and making art and teaching art are two of my absolute favorite things! I've been drawing since elementary school, and I've even completed a university degree in art. Through my experiences, I've learned how to draw in many different styles and with many different tools, but you don't need a degree in art or a lot of art supplies to draw!

One day, my 5-year-old son told me how frustrated he was with trying to draw. I told him that drawing is simple. The key is to be able to see the simple shapes that are hidden within the complex shapes.

This book shows you how to draw by beginning with simple shapes. Then, with my easy-to-follow, step-by-step instructions and helpful notes, you can add the details to finish a comic book character. There's even information throughout this book on making your own characters and comic books!

If you want a simple, approachable, and creative way to improve on your drawing skills, then you've picked up the right book!

–Spencer

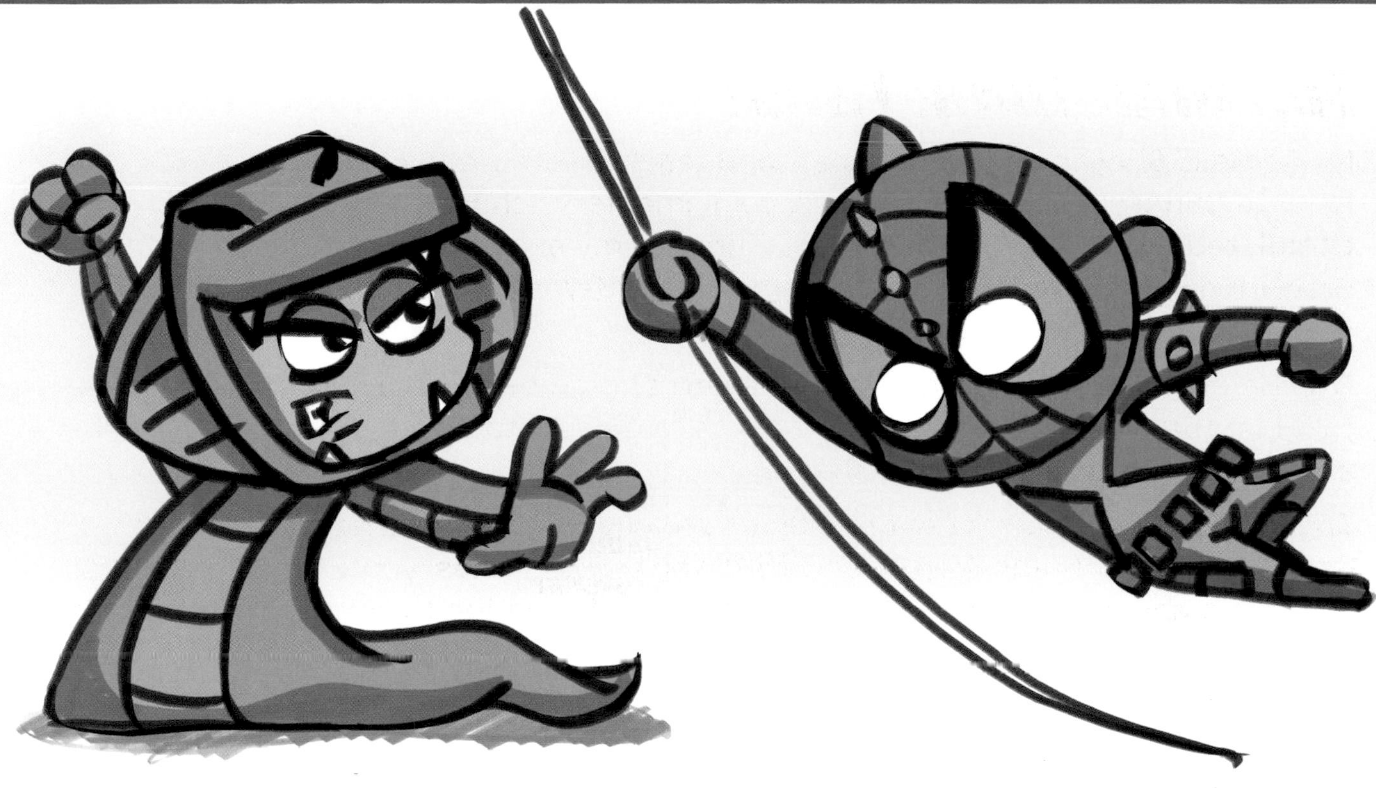

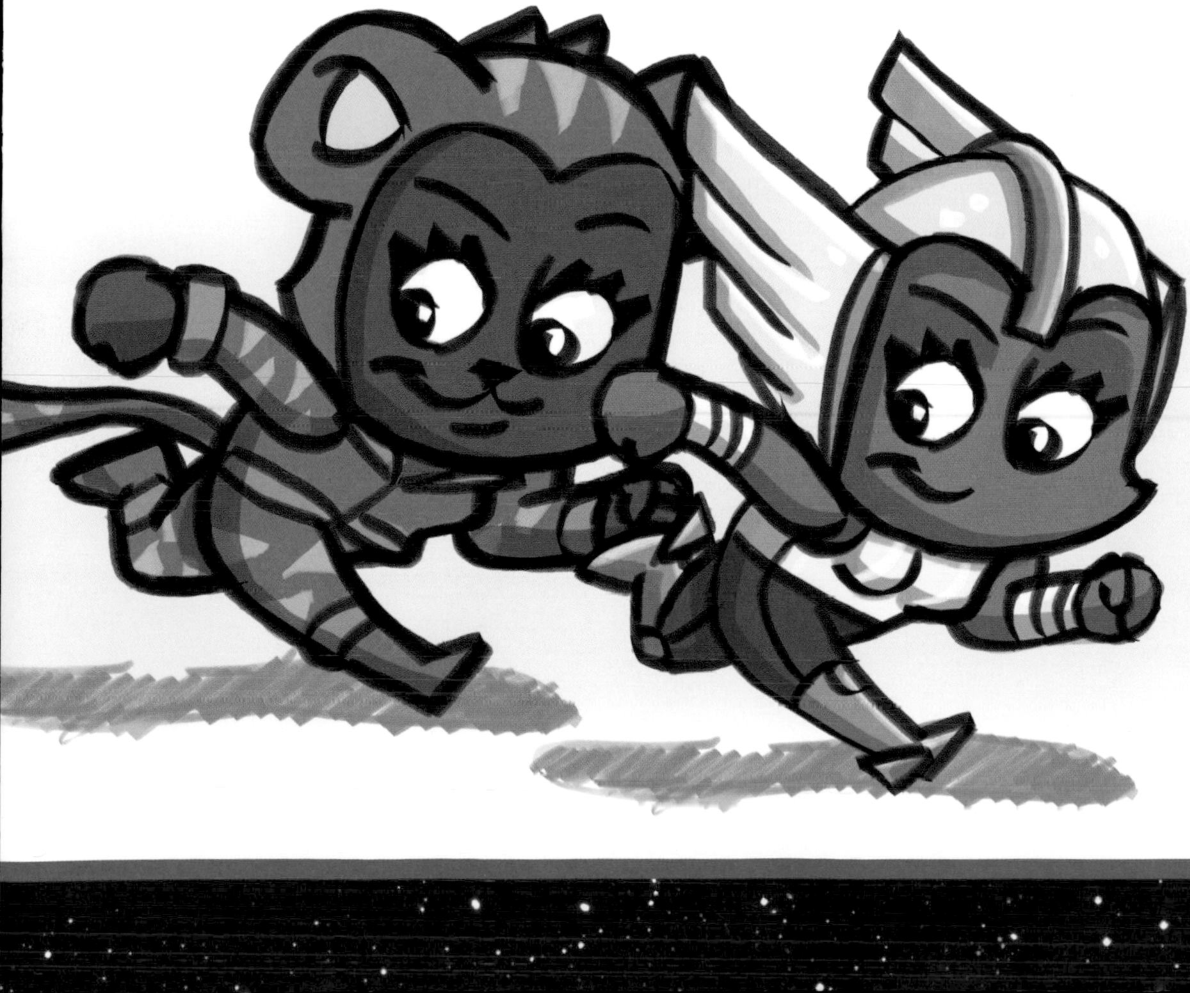

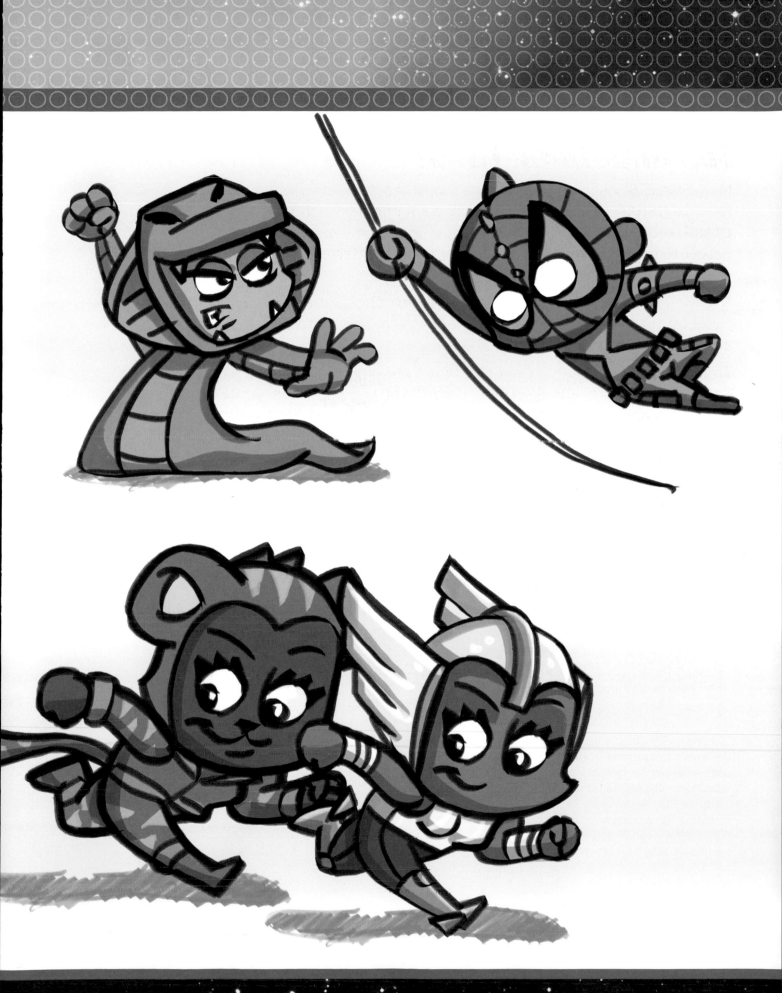

Tools & Materials

The artwork in this book was drawn and colored on a computer, but don't worry if you're not set up for that. You can create all of these comic book characters with traditional media, such as pencils, colored pencils, pens, crayons, and paints. Here are the supplies you may want to have handy to get started.

▶ **PAPER** Sketchpads and inexpensive printer paper are great for working out your ideas. Tracing paper is useful for tracing figures and creating a clean version of a sketch using a light box. Finally, cardstock is sturdier than thinner printer paper, which makes it ideal for drawing on repeatedly or for heavy-duty artwork.

▼ **BLACK FINE-LINE MARKER** Use a black fine-line marker to tighten your lines and add the finishing touch to your final color artwork.

▲ **PENCILS** Pencil lead, or graphite, varies in darkness and hardness. Pencils with a number and an H have harder graphite, which marks paper more lightly. Pencils with a number and a B mean the graphite is softer and looks darker on paper. Use H or HB pencils (HB pencils are equivalent to No. 2 pencils) for sketching exercises. In general, use harder pencils (H) for lighter, thinner lines. Use softer pencils (B) for bolder, thicker lines.

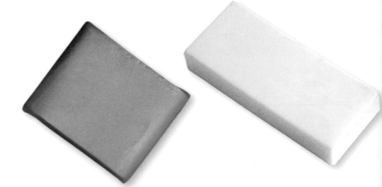

▼ **ERASERS** A vinyl eraser and a kneaded eraser are both good to have on hand. A vinyl eraser is white and rubbery; it's softer and gentler on paper than a pink eraser. A kneaded eraser is like putty in that you can mold it into shapes to erase small areas. You can also gently "blot" a sketch with a kneaded eraser to lighten the artwork.

▲ **PENS** Different inks work well for coloring. When buying pens, look for "waterproof" or "archival ink" printed on the side of the pen. Look for pens that release ink consistently for inking line art over sketches.

▼ **CIRCLE TEMPLATE** There are people out there who say that they can't even draw a circle! To make things easy, you can begin all the drawings in this book by tracing around something circular. This can be anything flat and circular that's not too big or too small. You could use a large coin (I use my own "Drawing Is Simple" coin at right, which has marks to help draw guidelines), a coaster, or a lid off of a jar. You can even buy shape templates at an art supply store or use a compass. Use the same circle template for each character so they will be proportionate to one another.

dis
DRAWINGisSIMPLE.com

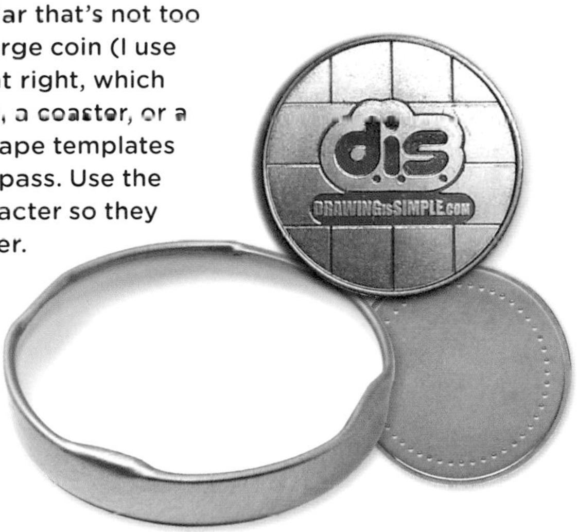

► **ART MARKERS**
Art markers are perfect for adding bold, vibrant color to your artwork. They are great for shading and laying down large areas of color.

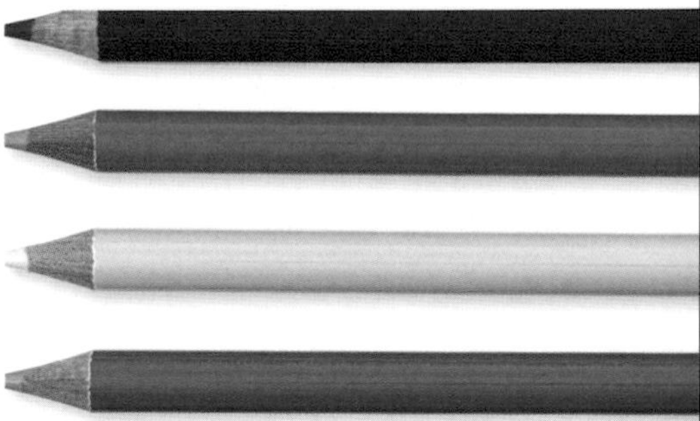

▲ **COLORED PENCILS**
Colored pencils layer over each other easily. They are user-friendly, and some are even erasable!

How to Use a Light Box

As its name suggests, a light box is a compact box with a transparent top and light inside. The light illuminates papers placed on top, allowing dark lines to show through for easy tracing. Simply tape your rough drawing on the surface of the light box. Place a clean sheet of paper over your original sketch and turn the box on. The light illuminates the drawing underneath and will help you accurately trace the lines onto the new sheet of paper. You can also create a similar effect by placing a lamp under a glass table or taping your sketch and drawing paper to a clear glass window and using natural light.

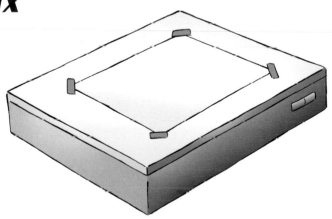

Drawing Basics

Absolutely everyone can draw! The easiest characters in this book are the forward-facing characters. To begin, you will draw just a few guidelines so you know where to place the major features of your character, including the head, eyes, body, and feet.

ON YOUR HEAD CIRCLE, MARK THE VERTICAL AND HORIZONTAL CENTERLINES. THESE GUIDELINES HELP DETERMINE WHERE TO PLACE THE CHARACTER'S EYES AND OTHER FACIAL FEATURES.

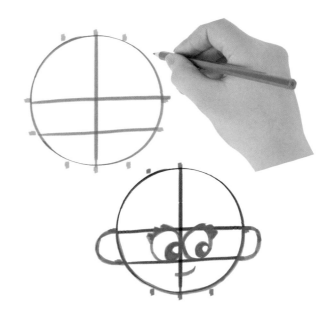

Start with Basic Shapes

The first circle is the character's head. For the body, draw a circle of the same size directly below the head. If you have trouble drawing circles, you can use a coin or something else that's flat and circular to trace a circle. With straight lines, mark other guidelines on your figure. If you have trouble drawing straight lines, use a ruler or another object with a straight edge.

TOP OF HEAD

EYES

BOTTOM OF HEAD

BODY

BOTTOM OF FEET

Draw Details

Now that you have the basic shapes and lines, it's time to add the details to your character. You'll add arms, legs, feet, hair, a costume, and maybe some accessories. But don't worry; even all the details are made up of basic shapes and lines. And each step in this book shows new lines in blue so you know exactly what to draw in each step.

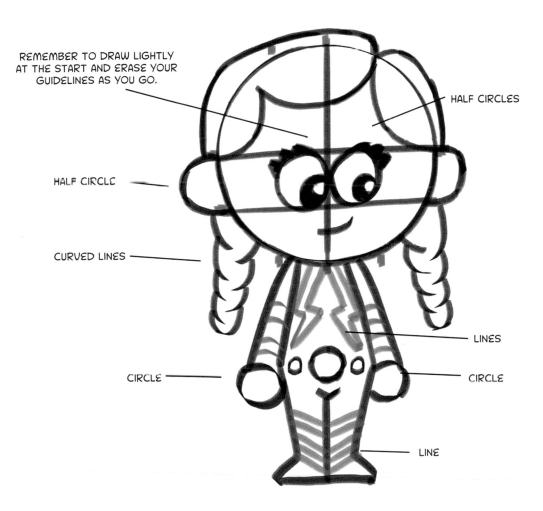

REMEMBER TO DRAW LIGHTLY AT THE START AND ERASE YOUR GUIDELINES AS YOU GO.

HALF CIRCLES

HALF CIRCLE

CURVED LINES

LINES

CIRCLE

CIRCLE

LINE

Did You Know?

The "head" count is a method in which the height of the head is used to measure the height of a figure. Because we are making small, supercute characters, most of the characters in this book are just two "heads" tall.

See? Drawing a forward-facing superhero is simple! After you're comfortable drawing characters head-on, kick things up a notch by drawing characters in action from different angles.

Start with Basic Shapes

Begin by drawing your guidelines. Because your character is not facing forward, you'll draw the guides in the face in different places. Draw a curved vertical and horizontal line on the head circle to indicate where the facial features will be. Also include lines in the body circle (or two circles if your character is very tall) to indicate where your character's torso and legs will be.

Draw Details

Now add details. Keep in mind the angle of the character and how the shapes would look from this view. Unlike the front view, a three-quarter view will not be symmetrical.

Add Color

Finish your character by adding color!

The Color Wheel

A color wheel is useful for understanding relationships between colors. Knowing where each color is located on the color wheel makes it easy to understand how colors relate to and react with one another.

Yellow
Yellow-Orange
Orange
Red-Orange
Red
Red-Purple
Purple
Blue-Purple
Blue
Blue-Green
Green
Yellow-Green

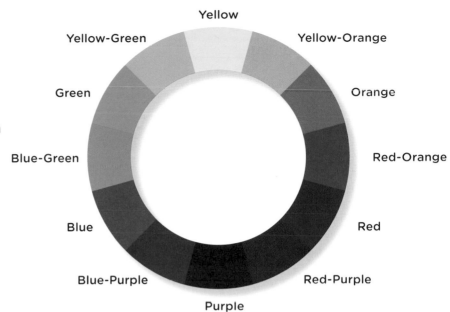

Easy Color Combinations

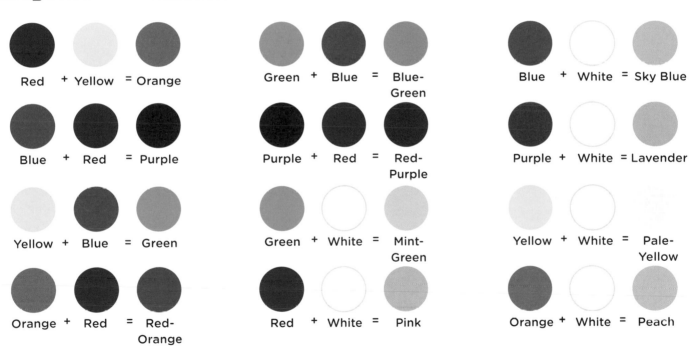

Red + Yellow = Orange
Blue + Red = Purple
Yellow + Blue = Green
Orange + Red = Red-Orange
Green + Blue = Blue-Green
Purple + Red = Red-Purple
Green + White = Mint-Green
Red + White = Pink
Blue + White = Sky Blue
Purple + White = Lavender
Yellow + White = Pale-Yellow
Orange + White = Peach

Adding Color to Your Drawing

Some artists draw directly on illustration board or watercolor paper and then apply color directly to the original pencil drawing; however, if you are a beginning artist, you might choose to preserve your original pencil drawing by making several photocopies and applying color to a photocopy. This way, you'll always have your original drawing in case you make a mistake or you want to experiment with different colors or mediums.

Captain Jinx Tagget

Backstory: Although her name is Jinx, Captain Jinx Tagget is not cursed with bad luck. In fact, she is quite lucky. Well, at least she has been ever since she found the Star Stone. She'd been crop-dusting in her dad's PA-36 plane when she saw a meteor crash into the field. She safely landed the plane and then circled back to examine the meteor. As soon as she touched the glowing stone buried within the meteor, it disappeared, and she could feel the glow in her hands. She soon realized that the Star Stone had given her powers.

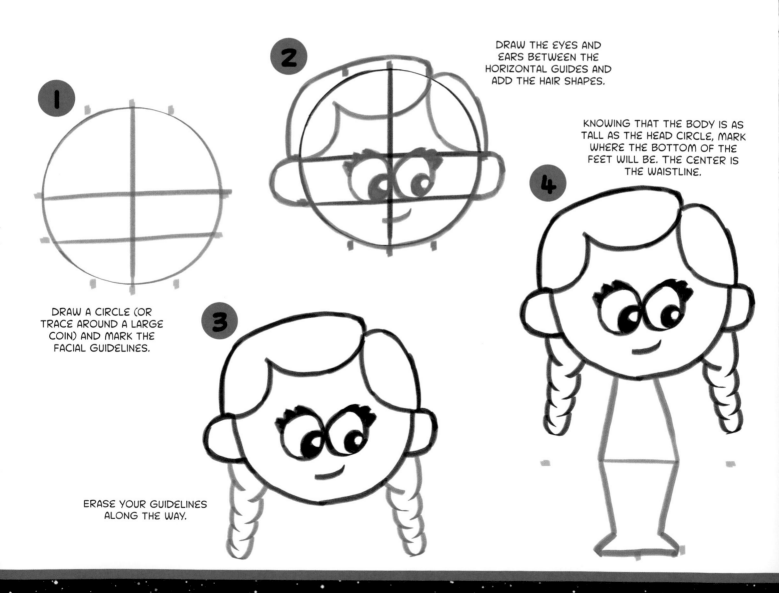

1. DRAW A CIRCLE (OR TRACE AROUND A LARGE COIN) AND MARK THE FACIAL GUIDELINES.

2. DRAW THE EYES AND EARS BETWEEN THE HORIZONTAL GUIDES AND ADD THE HAIR SHAPES.

3. ERASE YOUR GUIDELINES ALONG THE WAY.

4. KNOWING THAT THE BODY IS AS TALL AS THE HEAD CIRCLE, MARK WHERE THE BOTTOM OF THE FEET WILL BE. THE CENTER IS THE WAISTLINE.

Motivation: The more powers that Jinx discovers, the more she wants to know about the Star Stone and its origins.

Powers: Jinx can control gravity with energy pulses from her hands and use these abilities to fly.

Limitations: Unknown.

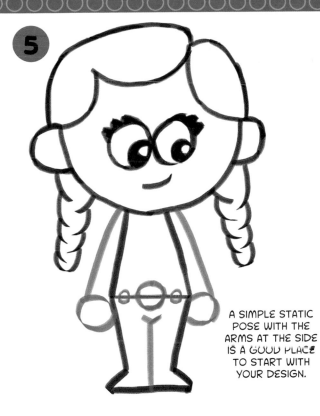

5

A SIMPLE STATIC POSE WITH THE ARMS AT THE SIDE IS A GOOD PLACE TO START WITH YOUR DESIGN.

6

7

ADD AN OUTLINE AND COLOR YOUR CHARACTER TO MAKE THE SHAPES POP OUT.

One of Jinx's unique abilities is her Star Blast. She can influence the power of gravity to stop criminals in their tracks and focus her powers to fly. In this action pose, you will show off Jinx's powers by having her fly and use her energy pulses.

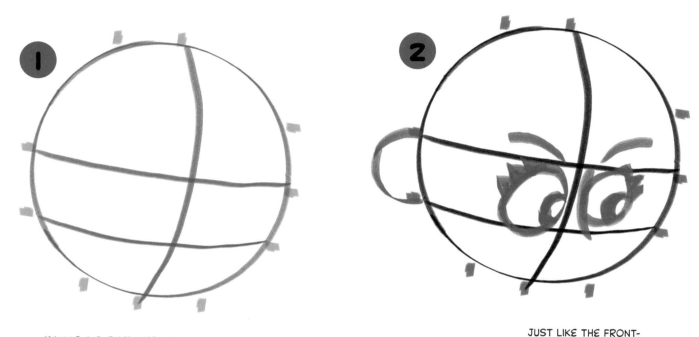

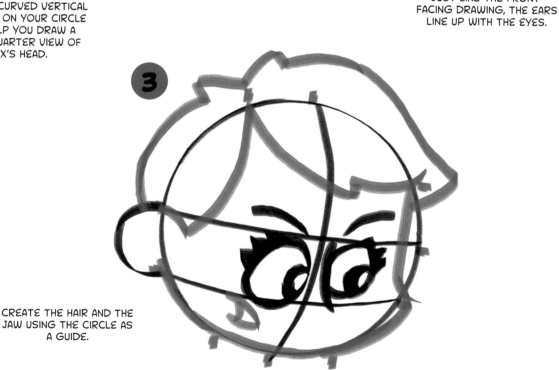

MAKING A CURVED VERTICAL GUIDELINE ON YOUR CIRCLE WILL HELP YOU DRAW A THREE-QUARTER VIEW OF JINX'S HEAD.

JUST LIKE THE FRONT-FACING DRAWING, THE EARS LINE UP WITH THE EYES.

CREATE THE HAIR AND THE JAW USING THE CIRCLE AS A GUIDE.

4

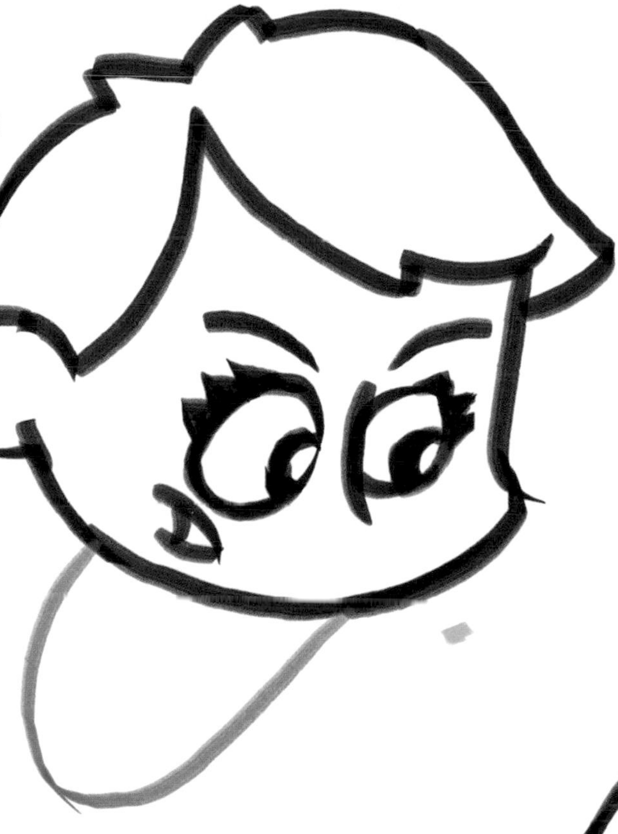

5

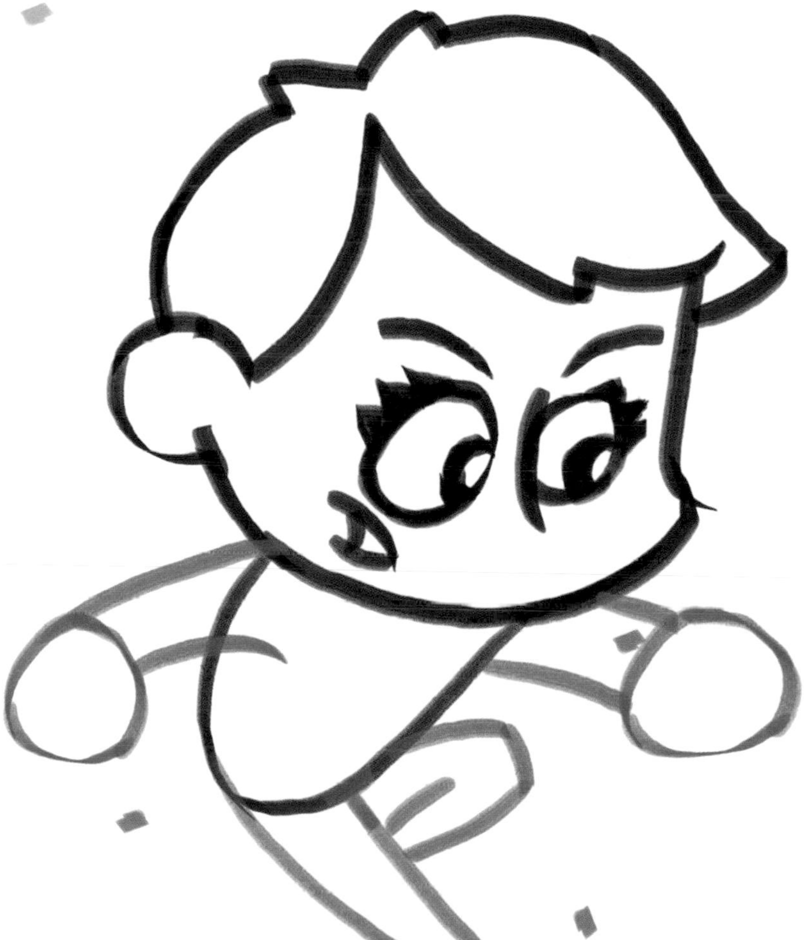

THE BODY HEIGHT IS ALMOST THE SAME AS THE HEAD HEIGHT. LIGHTLY ADD THE ARMS AND LEGS.

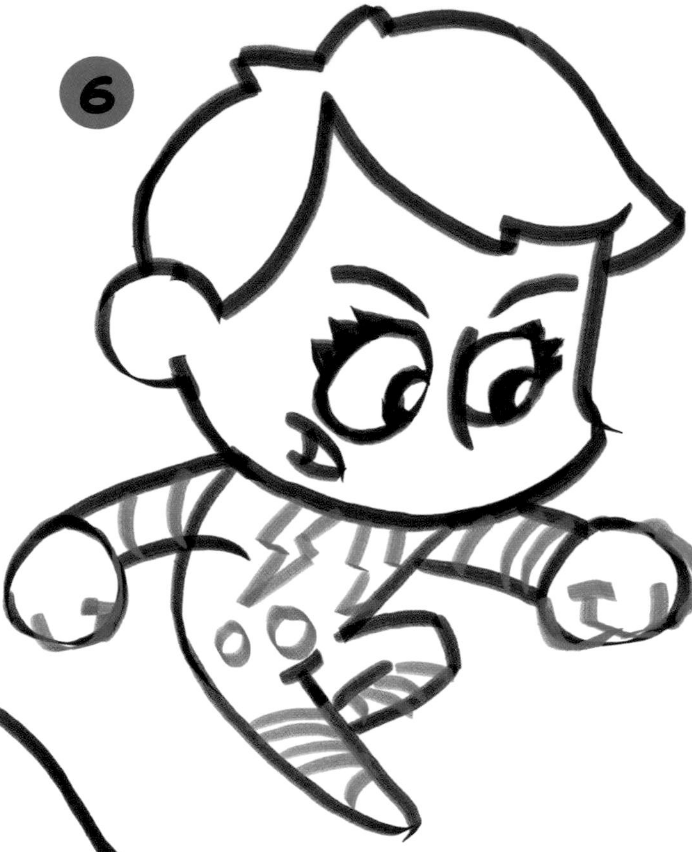
6

ADD THE SUIT AND HAND DETAILS.

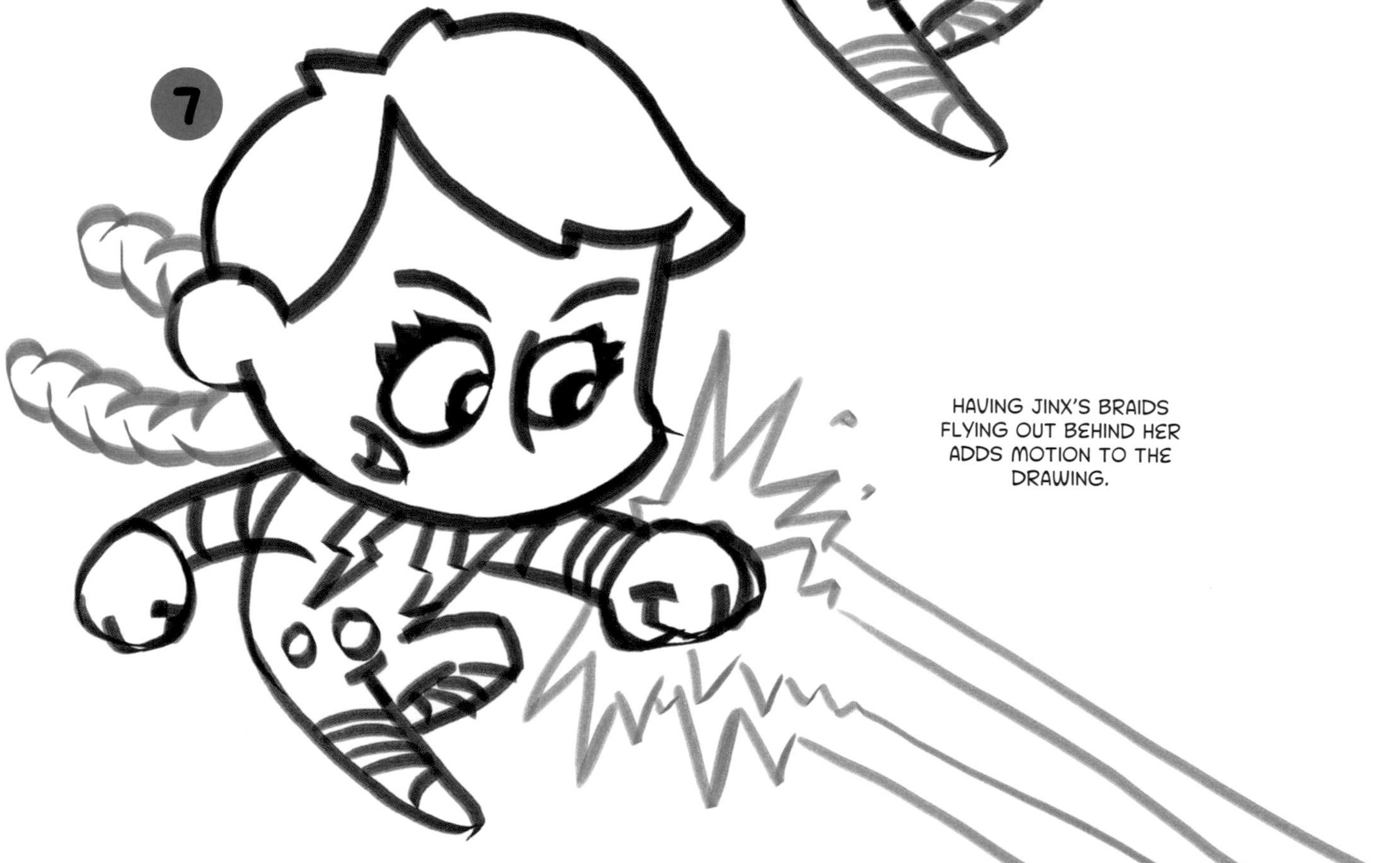
7

HAVING JINX'S BRAIDS FLYING OUT BEHIND HER ADDS MOTION TO THE DRAWING.

COLORS BRING THE CHARACTER TO LIFE! HAVE SOME FUN WITH THE HAND BEAM.

Prince Rogson

Backstory: Rogson was just a regular prince when his kingdom was attacked by Tazu the Terror. During the attack he learned from his father of an ancient power ring that had been kept secret by his family for generations. He has become the keeper of the Power of Erinth.

Motivation: Rogson's home world and his family were destroyed, and he seeks to ensure that the person responsible is brought to justice.

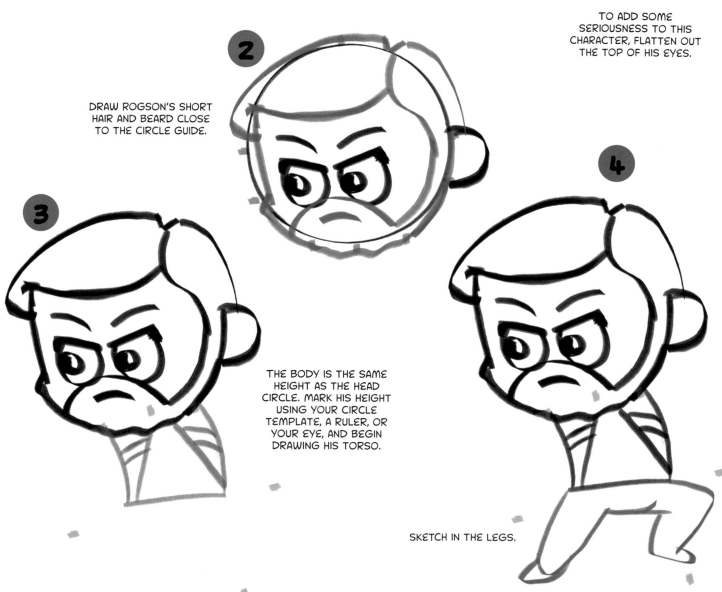

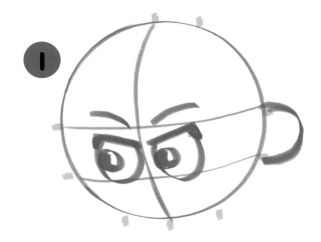

TO ADD SOME SERIOUSNESS TO THIS CHARACTER, FLATTEN OUT THE TOP OF HIS EYES.

DRAW ROGSON'S SHORT HAIR AND BEARD CLOSE TO THE CIRCLE GUIDE.

THE BODY IS THE SAME HEIGHT AS THE HEAD CIRCLE. MARK HIS HEIGHT USING YOUR CIRCLE TEMPLATE, A RULER, OR YOUR EYE, AND BEGIN DRAWING HIS TORSO.

SKETCH IN THE LEGS.

Powers: The power ring that Rogson possesses extends like a laser whip and can form into various shapes, either rigid or fluid.

Limitations: The ring has a limited power supply and length.

5

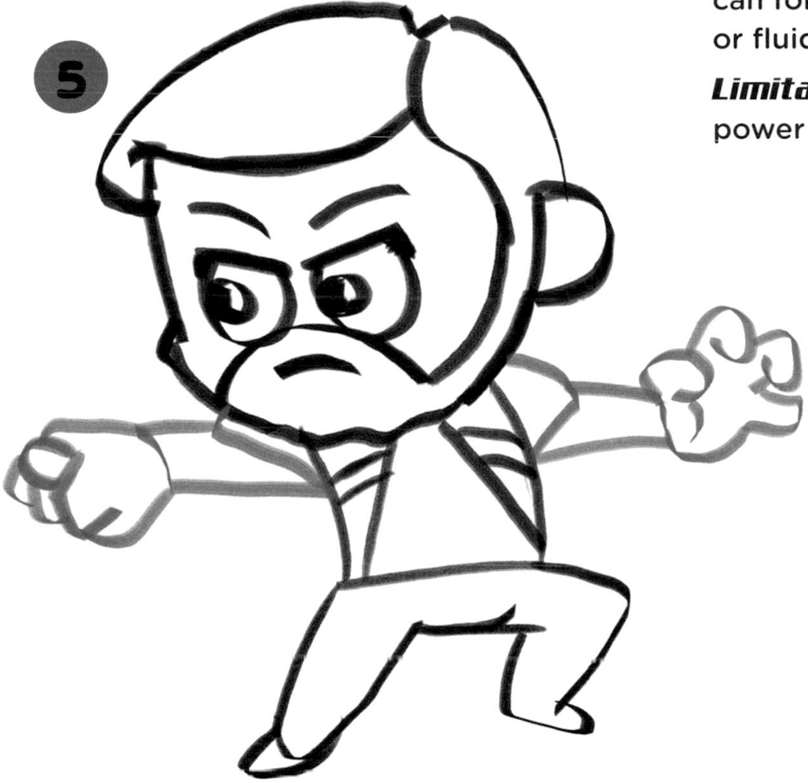

DON'T FORGET TO INCLUDE THE POWER RING ON ROGSON'S HAND.

6

THE COLOR PURPLE HAS BEEN ASSOCIATED WITH ROYALTY, POWER, AND WEALTH FOR CENTURIES, SO IT'S FITTING FOR PRINCE ROGSON'S COSTUME TO BE PURPLE AND GOLD.

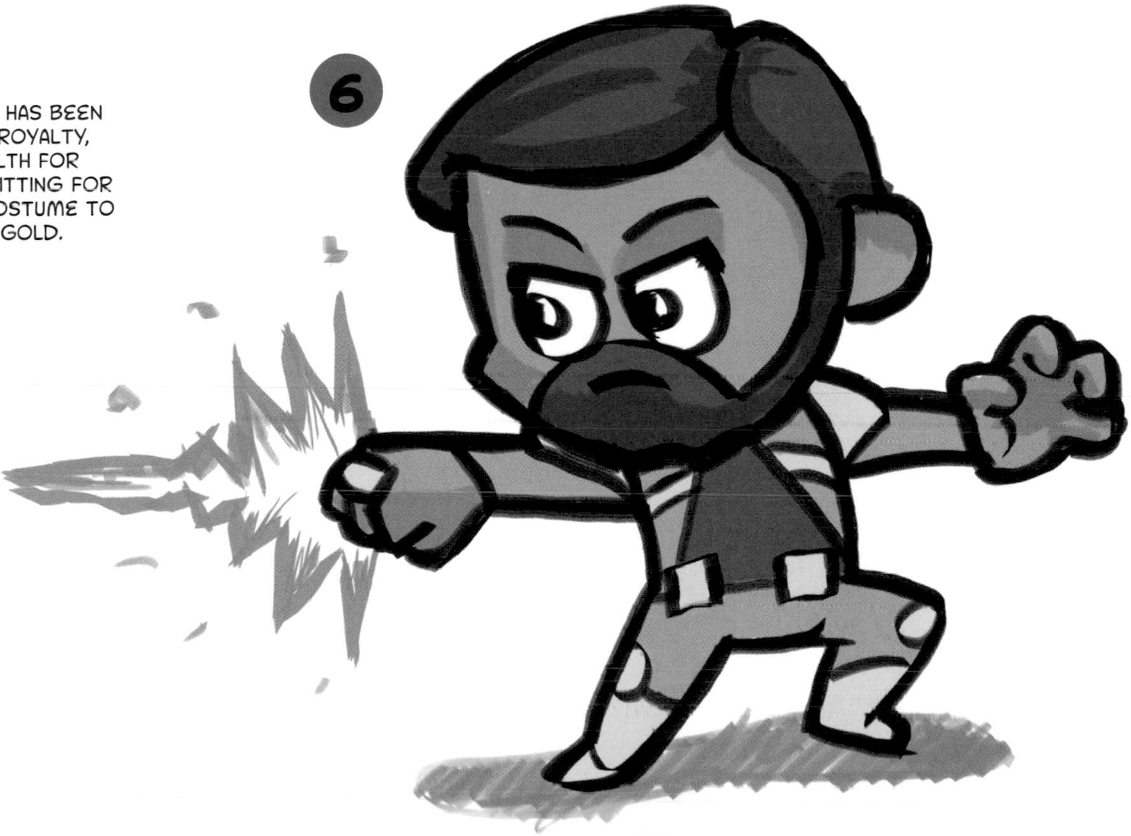

Creating a Hero

Comic book heroes, like Jinx Tagget, usually start out as normal, everyday people just like the rest of us, but there's something different, something special about them. We look up to heroes and want to see ourselves in them. We imagine that we too have that special quality.

Once they see the damage a villain has done, heroes are willing to sacrifice their own desires, their own needs, or even their own safety for the greater good. More than anything else, the heroes are willing to change. They grow and transform through their choices.

ONE OF THEIR GREATEST POWERS IS WISDOM

TRUSTWORTHY EYES

A HERO HAS A HEART

NEVER UNDERESTIMATE THE POWER OF AN AWESOME OUTFIT

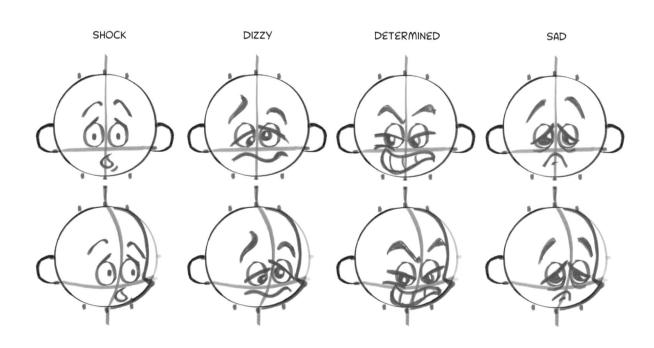

SHOCK DIZZY DETERMINED SAD

TRY SOME OF THESE POSES WITH YOUR HERO.

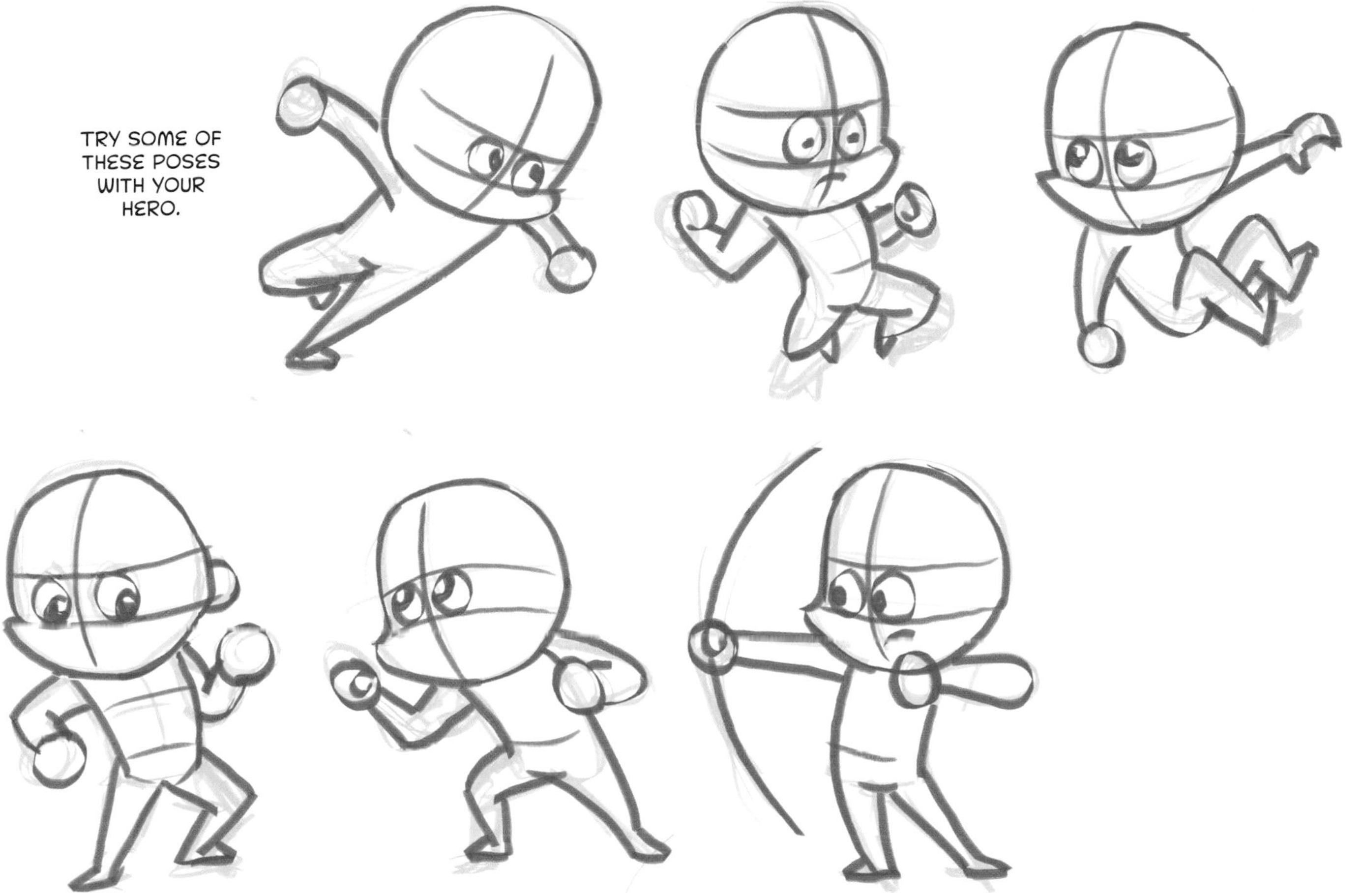

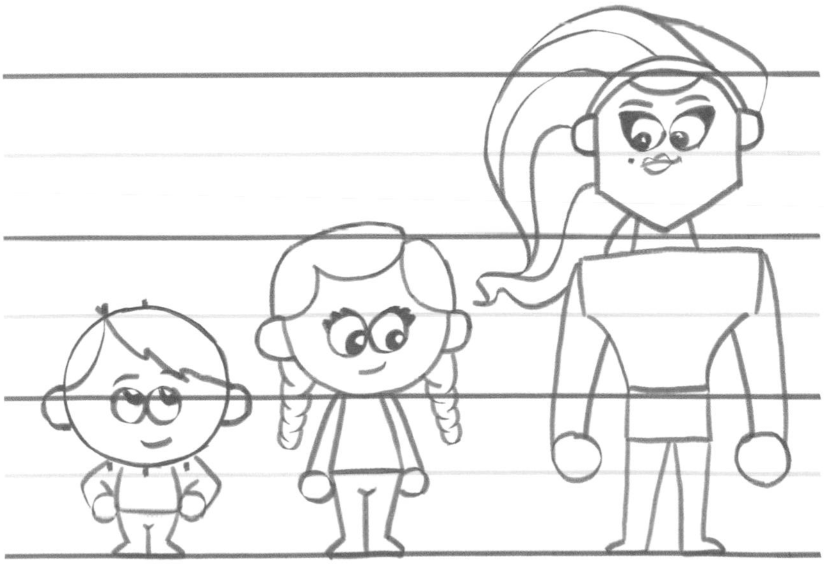

Heroes come in all shapes and sizes. Sure, they can be tall and have big muscles, but they can also look like the rest of us. Being relatable is one of the things that make us love heroes!

Make It Your Own!

While following the step-by-step projects in this book, feel free to personalize the characters. Change the costumes, hair, facial expressions, or colors. Here are just two examples of how you can change the Jinx Tagget projects on pages 12 and 14.

1

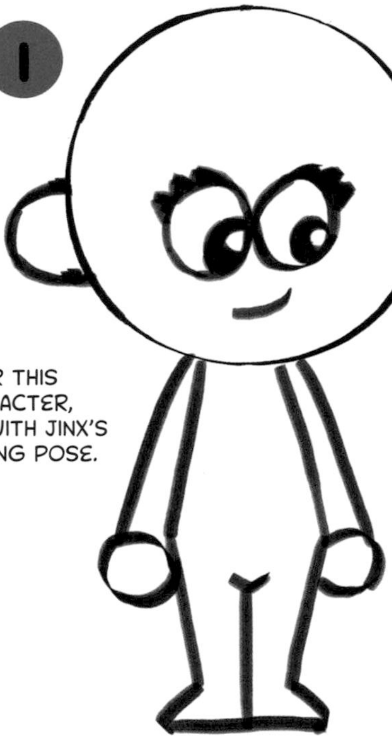

FOR THIS CHARACTER, START WITH JINX'S STANDING POSE.

2

HAVE SOME FUN AND CONTINUE THE SPACE THEME WITH A CLASSIC DESIGN—ADD BIG HAIR, FLARED GLOVES, AND SHOULDER PADS.

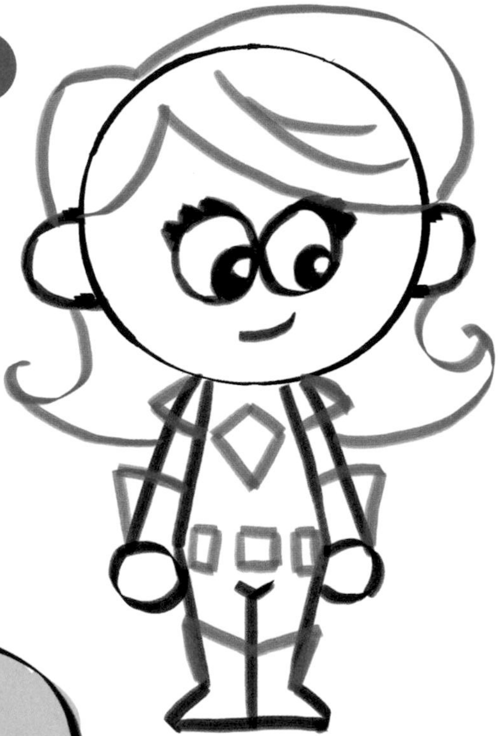

3

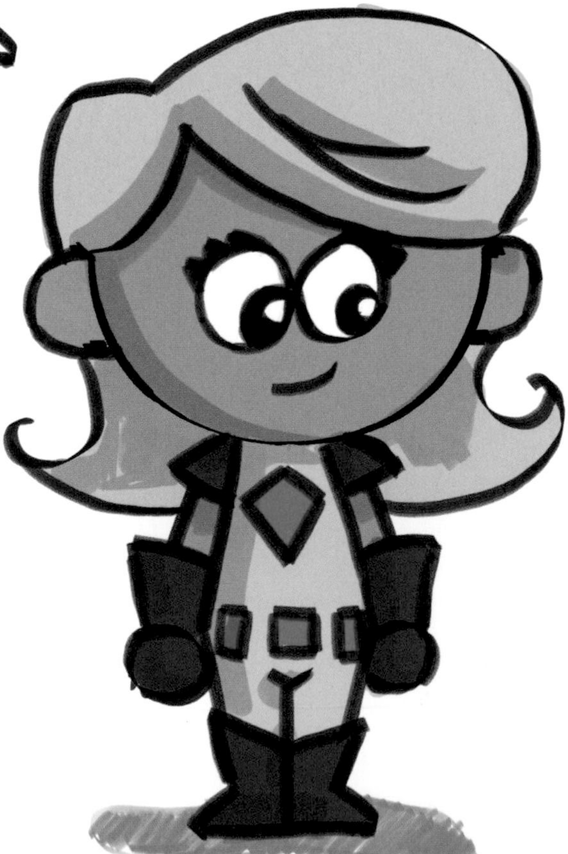

EXPERIMENT WITH YOUR COLOR CHOICES. PINK HAIR SEEMS TO BE THE PERFECT FIT FOR THIS CHARACTER!

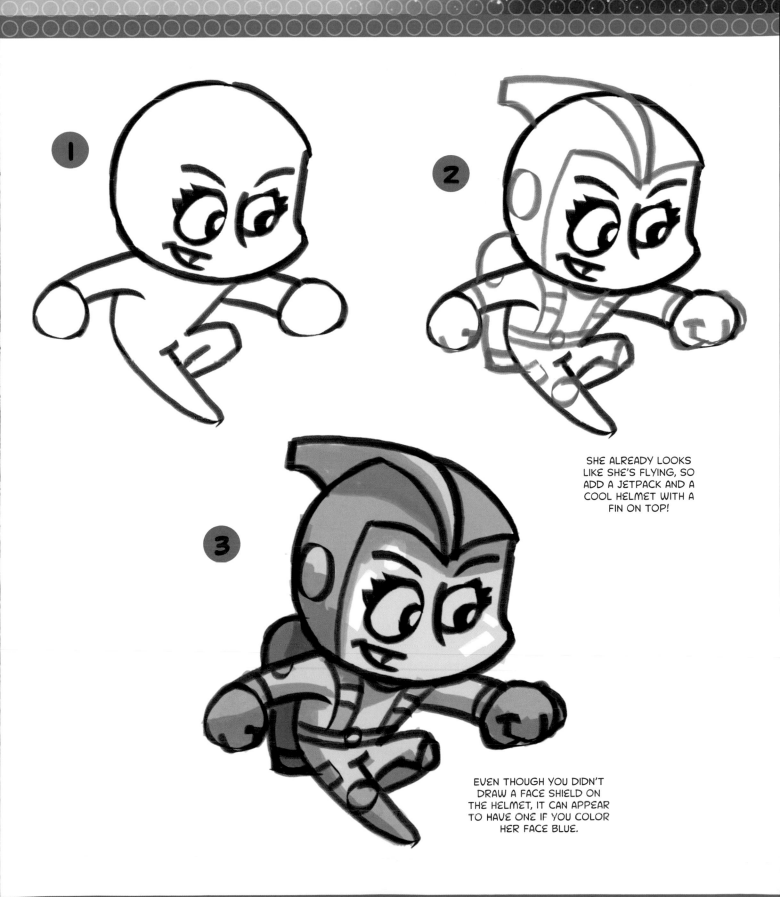

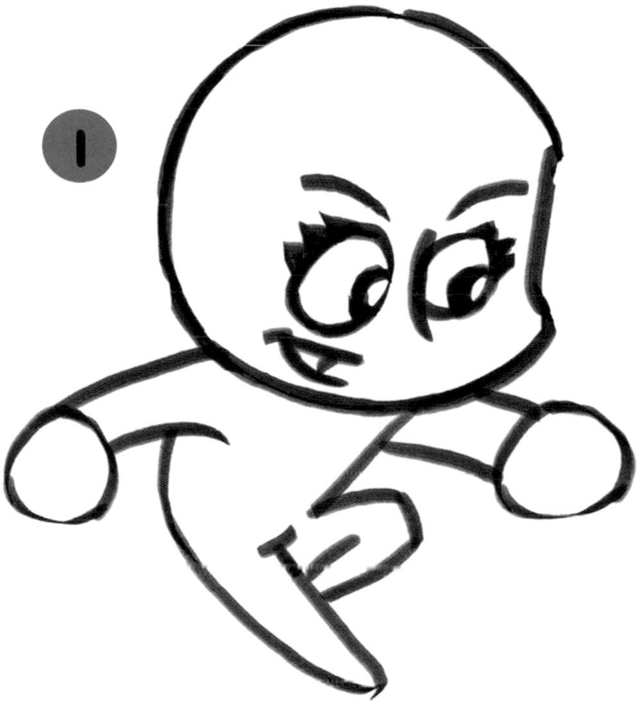
1

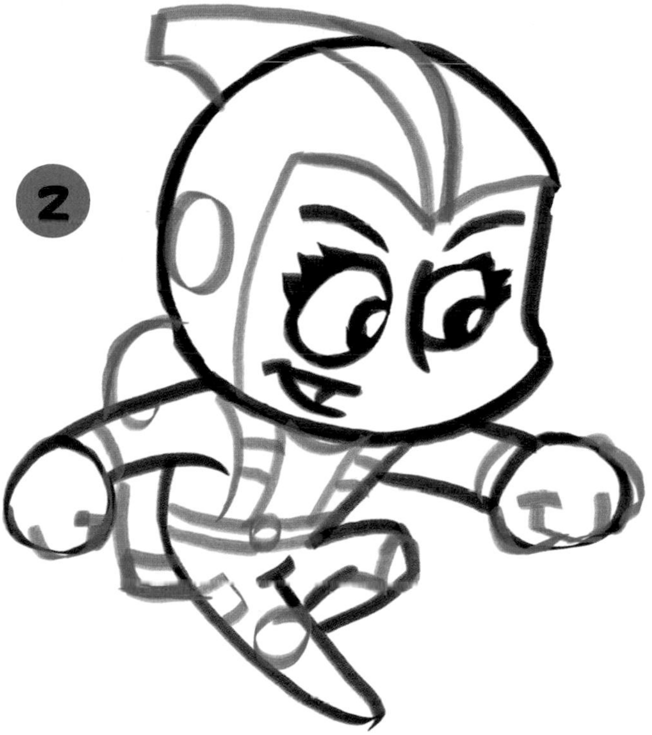
2

SHE ALREADY LOOKS LIKE SHE'S FLYING, SO ADD A JETPACK AND A COOL HELMET WITH A FIN ON TOP!

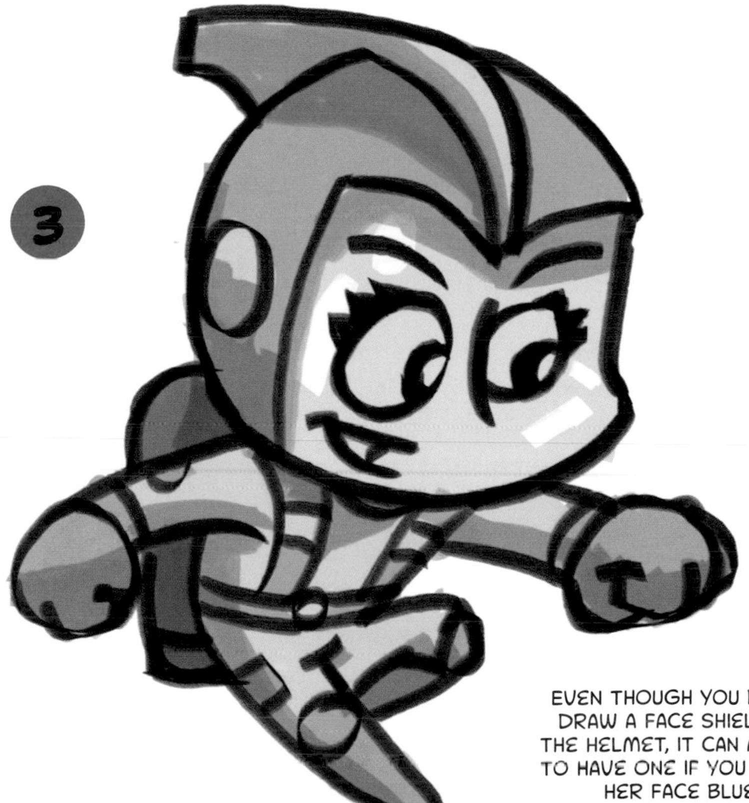
3

EVEN THOUGH YOU DIDN'T DRAW A FACE SHIELD ON THE HELMET, IT CAN APPEAR TO HAVE ONE IF YOU COLOR HER FACE BLUE.

Tazu the Terror

Backstory: Not much is known about the history of Tazu the Terror. He first came to prominence in the Battle of Gillan. It would appear that he was the lone survivor of the Kanto Siege and was thrust into a position of authority. He wore the mantle well and swiftly took command of all the attacking forces.

Motivation: Tazu seeks to bring order to the chaos that he sees in the galaxy.

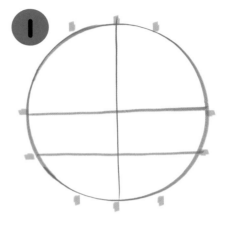

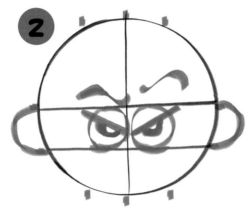

TAZU HAS EXPRESSIVE EYES AND EYEBROWS.

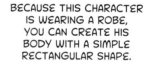

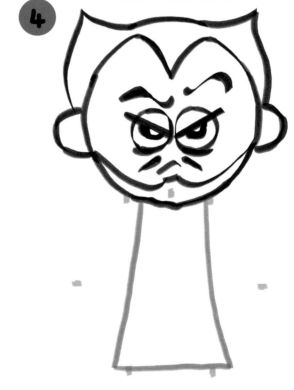

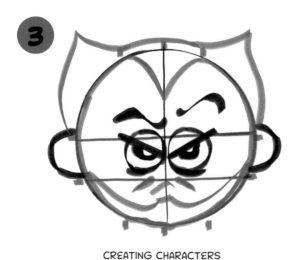

CREATING CHARACTERS WITH A UNIQUE LOOK LIKE THIS WILL HELP THEM STAND OUT IN A CROWD.

BECAUSE THIS CHARACTER IS WEARING A ROBE, YOU CAN CREATE HIS BODY WITH A SIMPLE RECTANGULAR SHAPE.

Powers: Tazu's staff has magical properties, but his greatest power is his keen intellect and the ability to accurately predict the actions of his foes.

Limitations: His absolute drive for justice has cursed Tazu with limited vision, and he can only see the world in black and white.

5

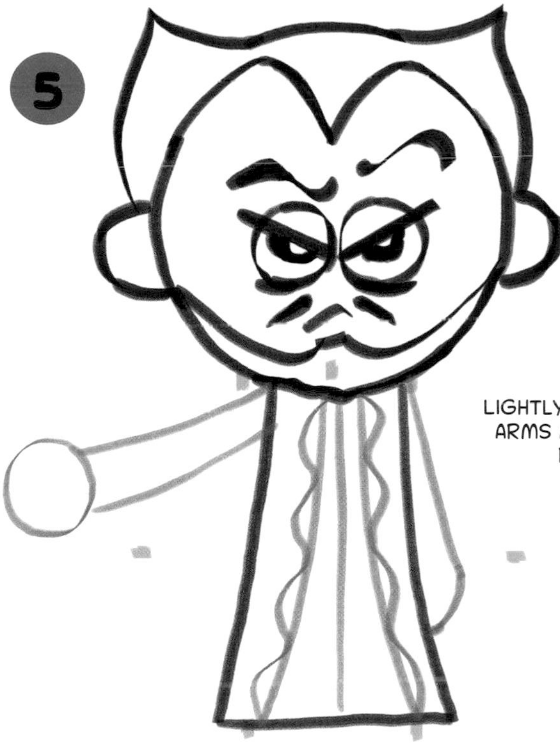

LIGHTLY SKETCH IN THE ARMS AND THE ROBE DETAILS.

6

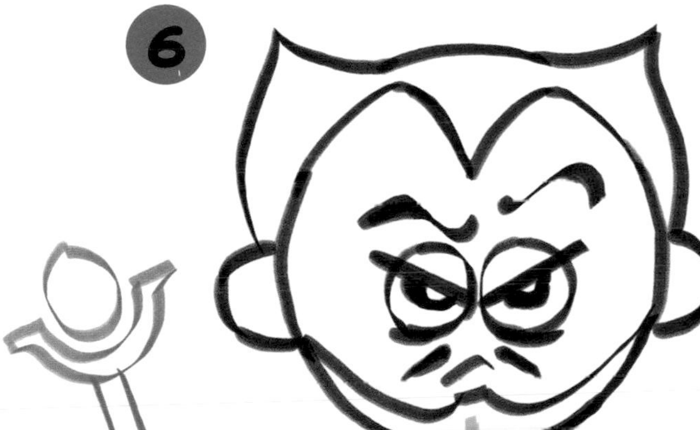

ADD MORE DETAILS AND TAZU'S MAGIC STAFF. BE SURE TO EXTEND THE STAFF ALL THE WAY TO THE GROUND.

7

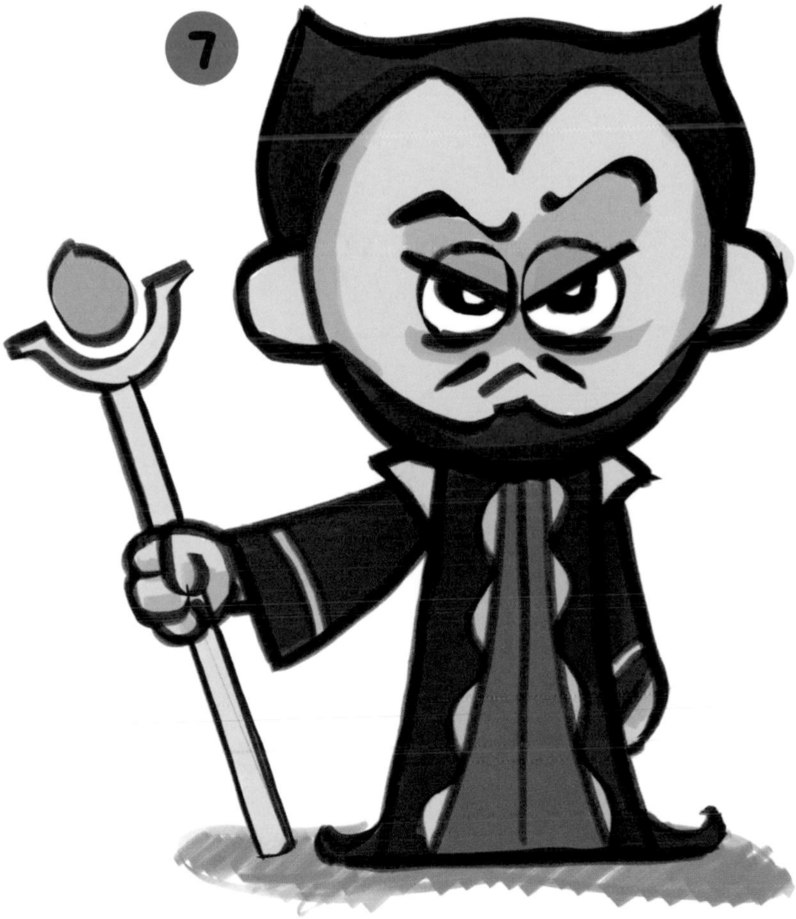

Now that you have a good understanding of Tazu the Terror's design and the style of his outfit, you can make more dynamic action poses, such as him wielding his magical staff! Tazu is never far from his magical staff. The mysterious gem at the head of the staff seems to have a mind of its own as it floats above the mounting prongs.

1

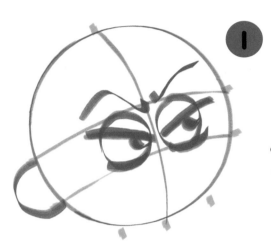

TO ADD A NEW DYNAMIC TO THE POSE, ANGLE THE CHARACTER'S HEAD UP BY ROTATING YOUR HORIZONTAL AND VERTICAL CENTERLINES.

2

ADD DETAILS TO YOUR GUIDELINES AND THEN ERASE THEM.

3

FOR DYNAMIC MOTION, ADD AN EXTREME BEND TO THE RECTANGLE THAT MAKES UP TAZU'S ROBE SHAPE.

LIGHTLY SKETCH IN HIS ARMS AND HANDS AND ADD DETAILS TO THE ROBE.

4

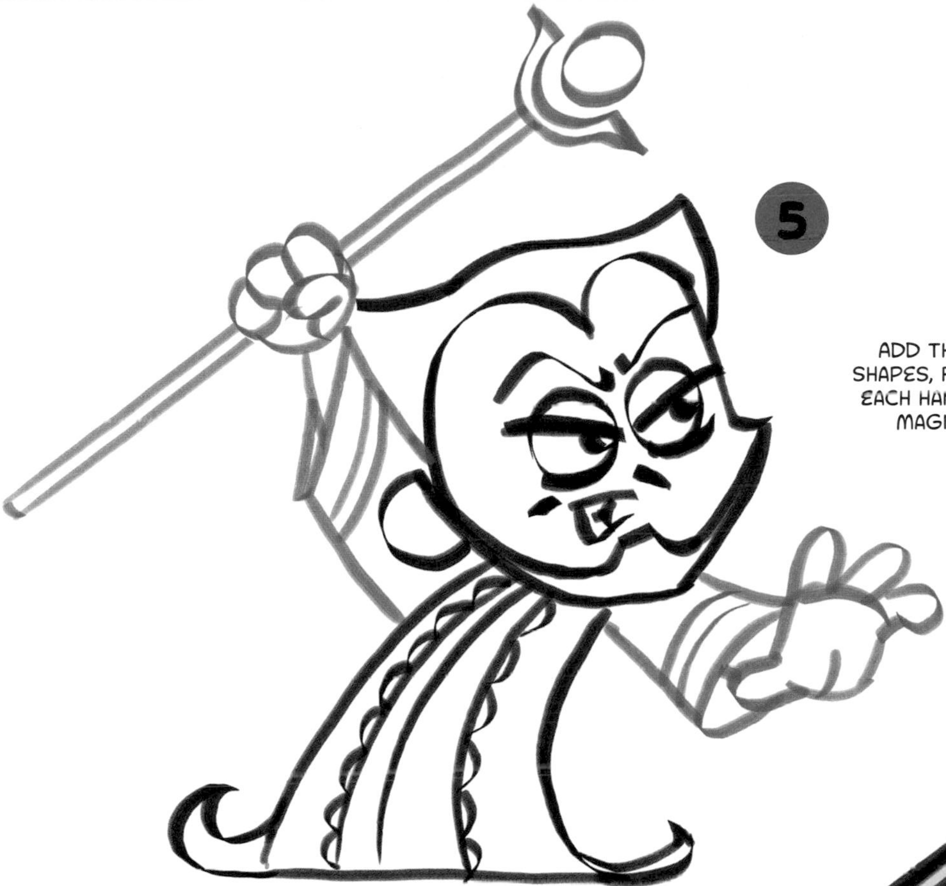

5

ADD THE SLEEVE SHAPES, FINGERS FOR EACH HAND, AND THE MAGIC STAFF.

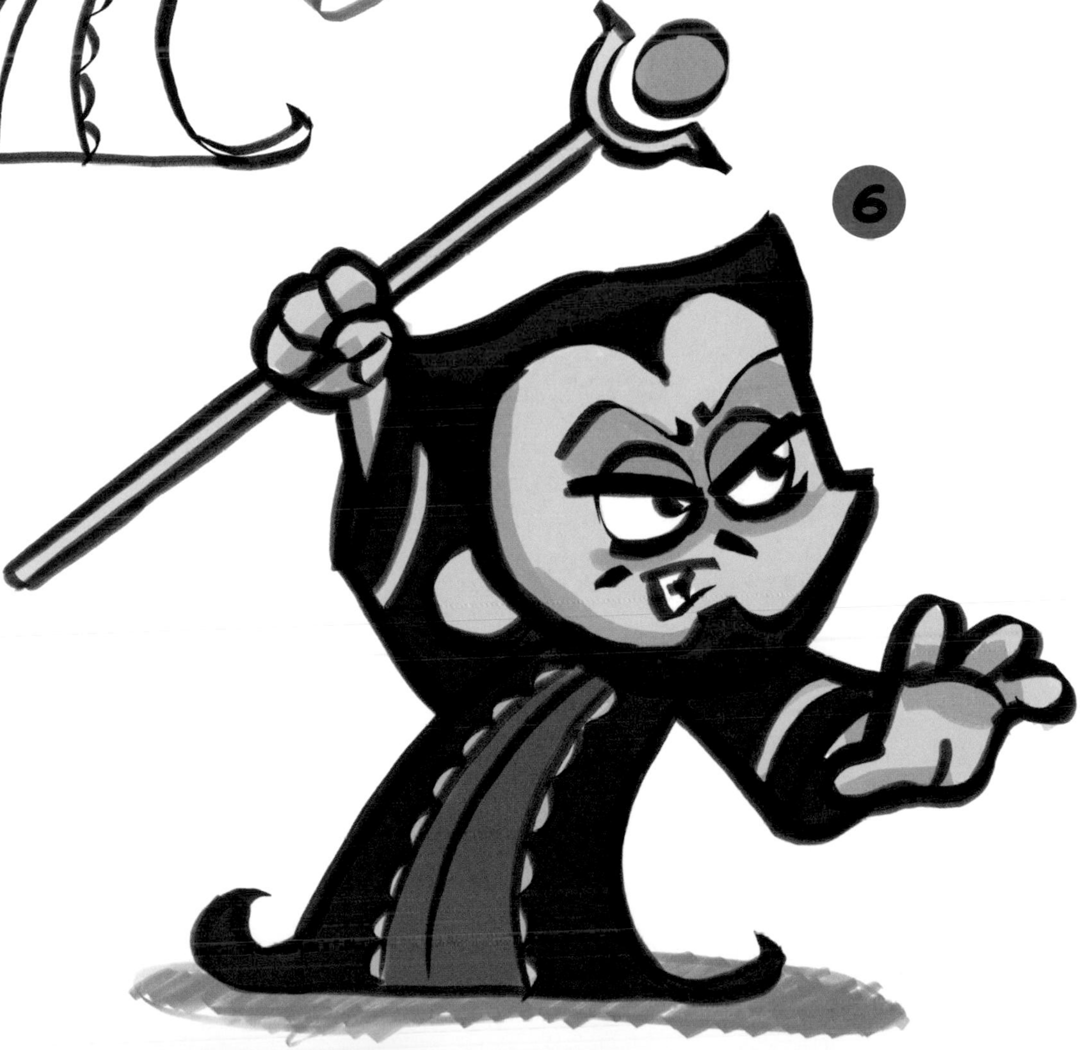

6

Eyeris

Backstory: Eyeris is a dedicated but unambitious villain. If she's not on the clock, she's not working. Other than that, her history is her own, and we're all anxious to see what happens when she cashes her final paycheck.

Motivation: Eyeris is only in it for the money. She works for the highest bidder to amass her wealth, but no one knows what she's doing with it.

1

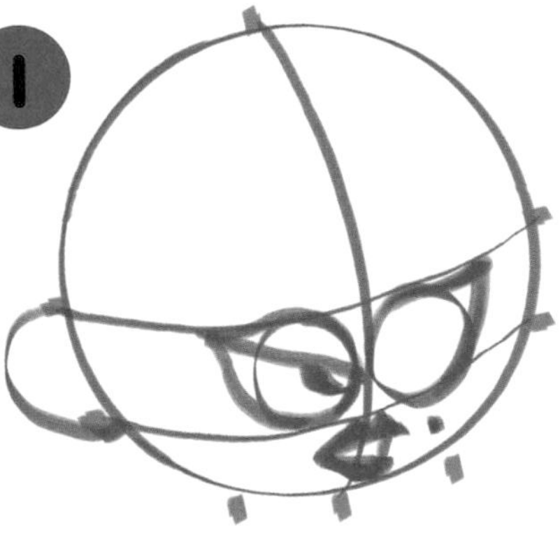

2

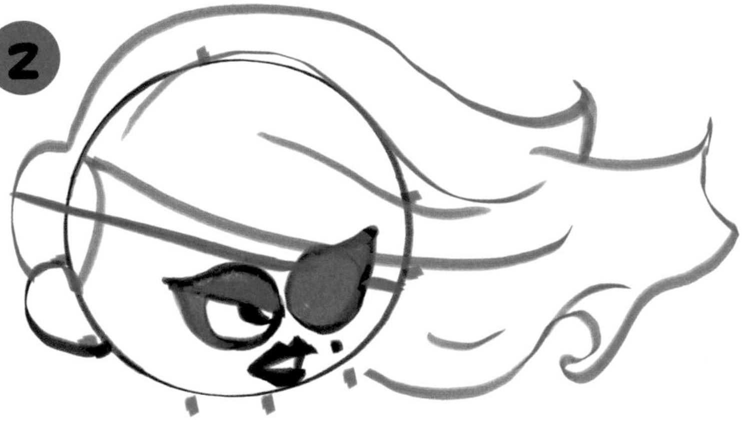

IN ADDITION TO THE BIG, FLOWING HAIR, ANOTHER WAY TO EMPHASIZE THE DYNAMIC POSE IS TO HAVE THE BODY MOVING IN THE OPPOSITE DIRECTION OF THE HAIR.

3

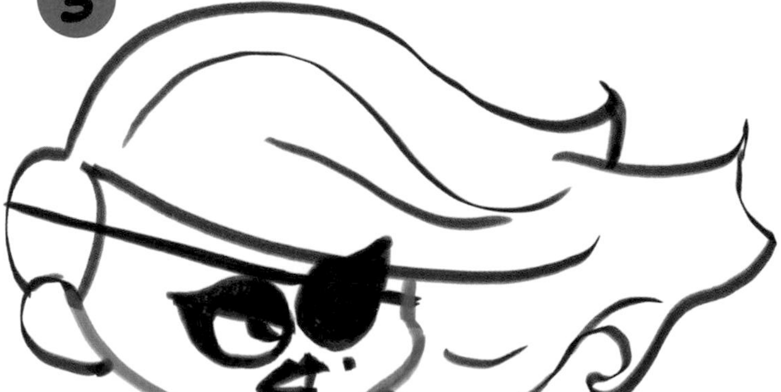

4

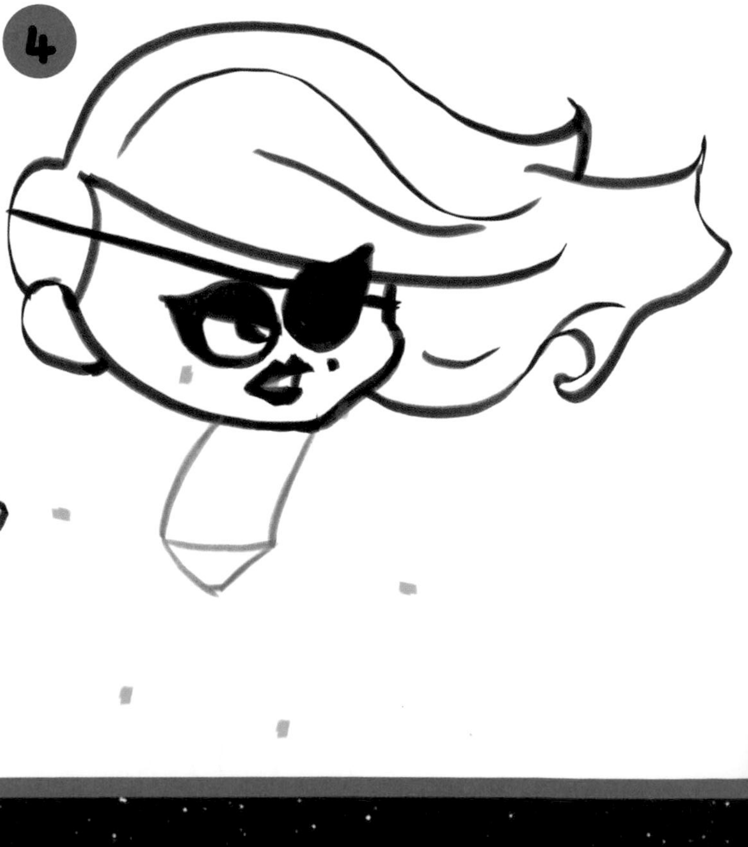

Powers: A photographic memory means that she can easily pick up any skill set. It also means that she holds a wicked grudge.

Limitations: Somewhere under that rough exterior, there's a chance that Eyeris might do the right thing.

5

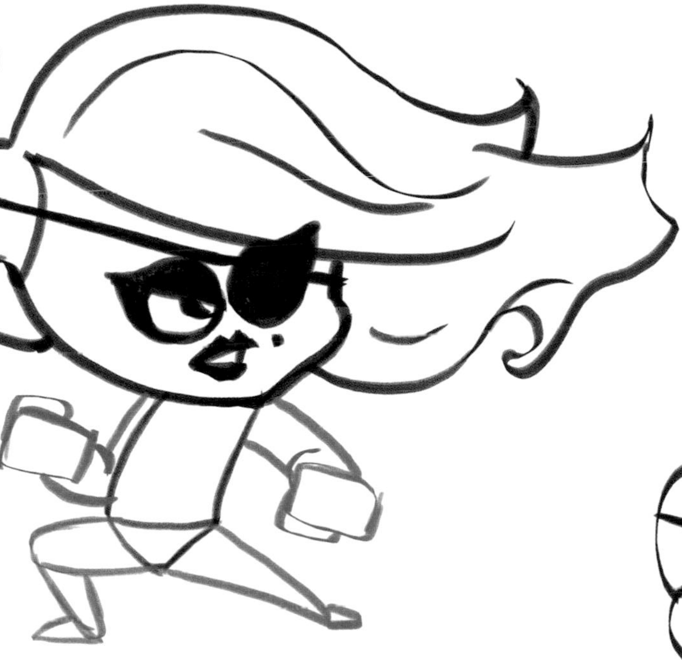

SKETCH OUT THE ARMS AND LEGS AND ADD DETAILS TO THE CHARACTER'S OUTFIT.

6

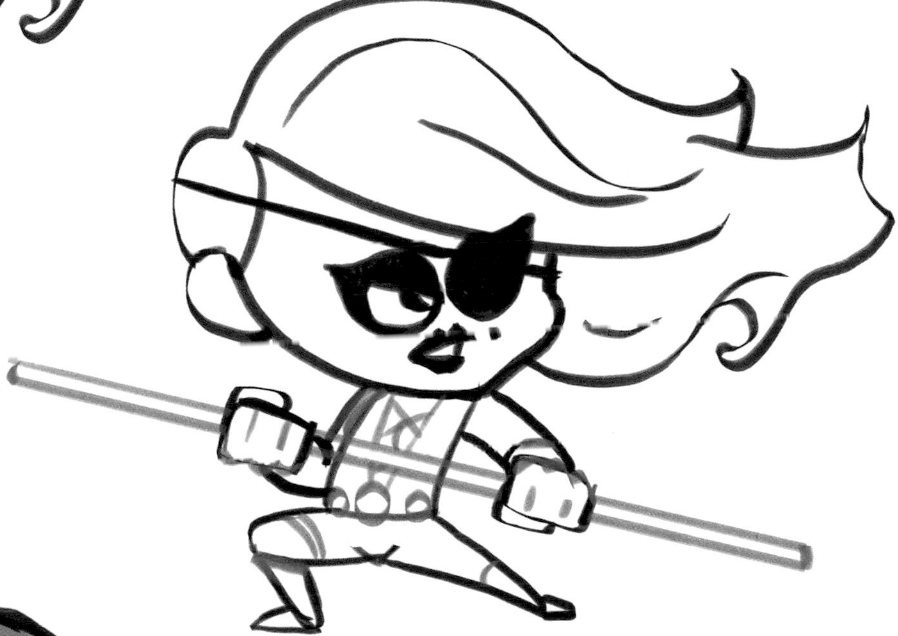

7

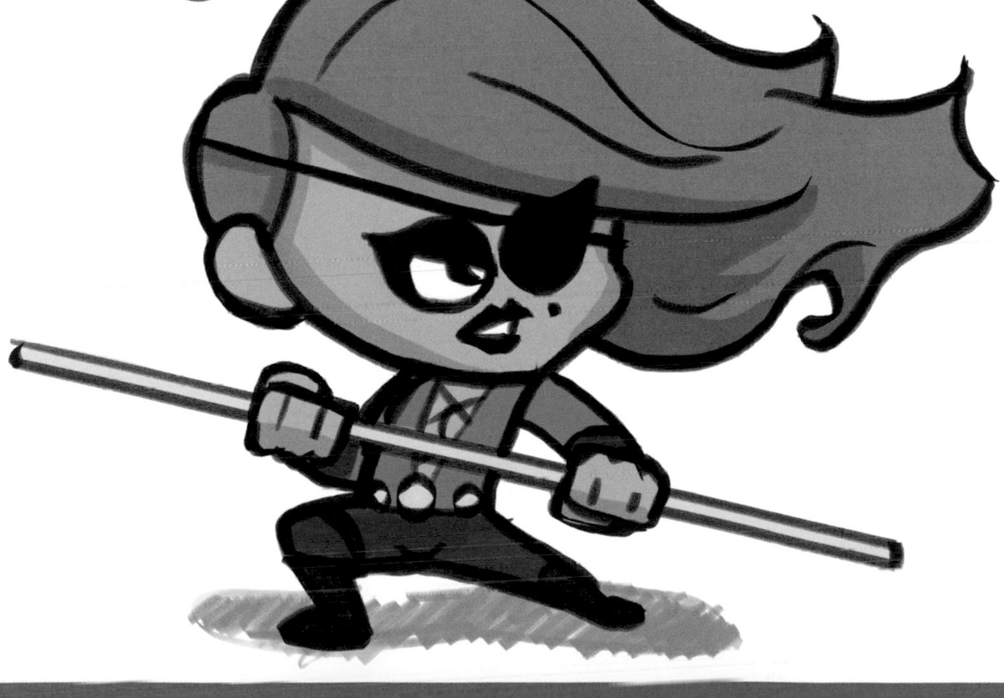

Creating a Villain

When creating your own cast of characters for a comic book, start with the villain. While the hero is the superstar of the story, remember that without a villain, there would be nothing for your hero to fight against! Starting with the villain helps to create the world that your hero lives in. This character will introduce elements of conflict that your hero has to overcome and will provide a driving force for your hero's actions.

Your hero is only as compelling as the villain he or she is fighting against, and the greatest villains are the heroes' superiors. The villain is the reason that the story begins, and the hero is the reason that it ends!

To the right is Tazu the Terror. Turn to page 24 to learn more about his backstory, motivation, powers, and limitations—and to learn how to draw him!

SLICKED-BACK HAIR

HEAVY EYELIDS

EXPRESSIVE EYEBROWS

ANGRY EYES

DARK LINES UNDER EYES

FACIAL HAIR

IN PLACE OF INNER STRENGTH, THE VILLAIN WILL OFTEN HAVE SOME SORT OF POWERFUL ACCESSORY

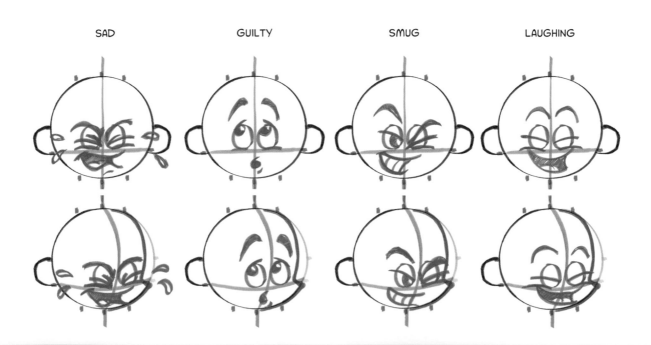

SAD   GUILTY   SMUG   LAUGHING

Physical Appearance: Many villains can be identified by some of their physical characteristics. Think about adding facial scars or other signs of injuries and wounds. A strange tattoo may hint at a mysterious or troubled past. Consider these characteristics when making your own villain.

TRY SOME OF THESE
POSES WITH YOUR VILLAIN.

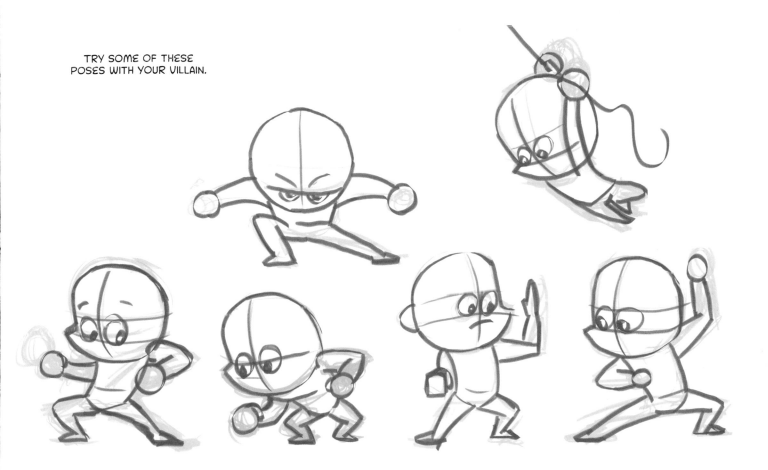

Backstory: Some villains are scarred from a terrible childhood and are now living in an underground lair, bent on world domination. But what makes an intriguing, unique villain? Not all villains are pure evil. Remember that villains are actually the heroes of their own stories. They have motives and reasons for their evil actions. Develop your villain's backstory, motivations, powers, and limitations so he or she is a formidable foe for your hero.

Don't forget the minions and sidekicks! Villains surround themselves with other people to do their dirty work. What kind of minion would choose to be associated with your villain, and why?

Monsclara

Backstory: The Monsclara are a powerful but clumsy race from the planet Marumei. They prefer a quiet and peaceful existence, but they are fiercely defensive of their clan and village.

Motivation: Live, laugh, love. They are simple creatures with simple cares.

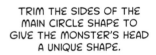

FOR THIS MONSTER, SHIFT THE EYELINE ABOVE THE CENTER HORIZONTAL LINE. THIS WILL GIVE THE CHARACTER A LARGER CHIN AND STRONGER APPEARANCE.

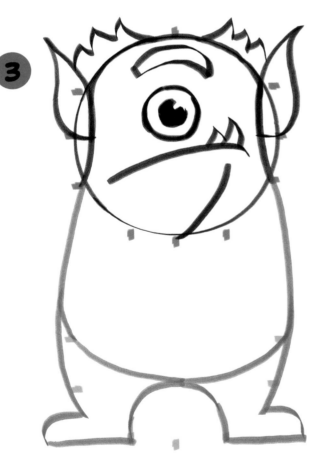

TRIM THE SIDES OF THE MAIN CIRCLE SHAPE TO GIVE THE MONSTER'S HEAD A UNIQUE SHAPE.

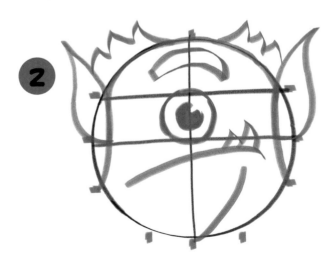

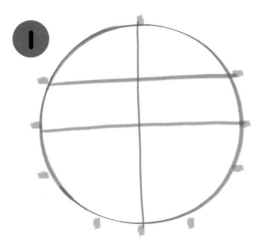

THE BODY IS AS TALL AS AND SLIGHTLY WIDER THAN THE HEAD CIRCLE.

MAKE THIS CHARACTER'S ARMS HUGE! THEN SKETCH IN SOME SPOTS THROUGHOUT THE BODY.

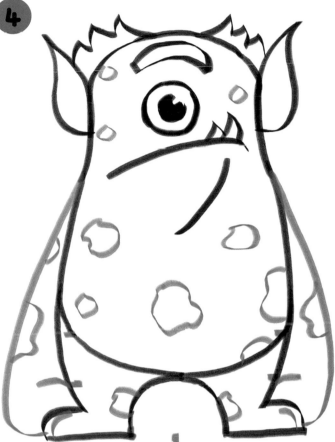

Powers: The Monsclara have an uncanny ability to see the aura projected by other living beings. This ability allows them to better know the true intentions of those they interact with.

Limitations: Depth perception.

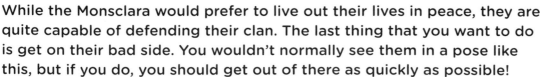

While the Monsclara would prefer to live out their lives in peace, they are quite capable of defending their clan. The last thing that you want to do is get on their bad side. You wouldn't normally see them in a pose like this, but if you do, you should get out of there as quickly as possible!

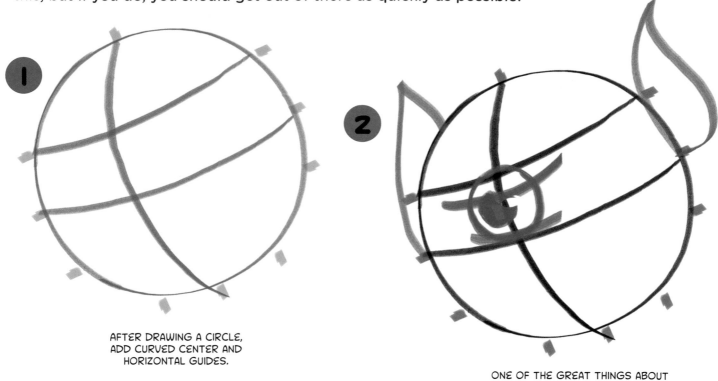

AFTER DRAWING A CIRCLE, ADD CURVED CENTER AND HORIZONTAL GUIDES.

ONE OF THE GREAT THINGS ABOUT A MONSTER WITH A SINGLE EYE IS THAT YOU'LL ALWAYS KNOW EXACTLY WHERE TO PLACE IT ON THE GUIDELINES—RIGHT IN THE CENTER!

4

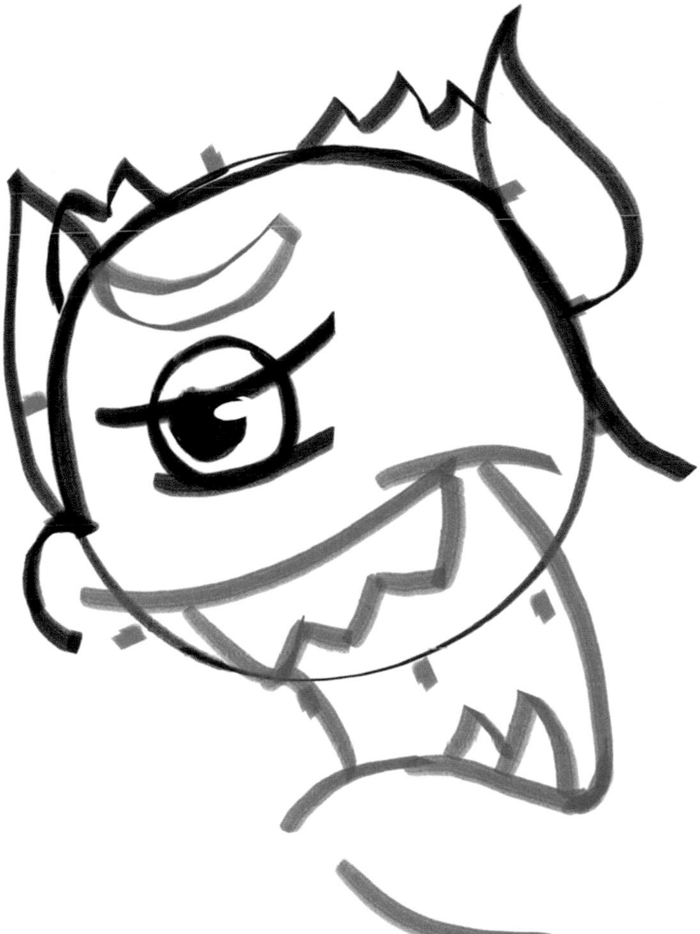

DRAW THE EYEBROW AND ADD THE BIG, OPEN MOUTH. START WITH SMILE LINE ON TOP; THEN ADD THE TOP TEETH, AND FINISH WITH THE LOWER LIP AND BOTTOM TEETH.

5

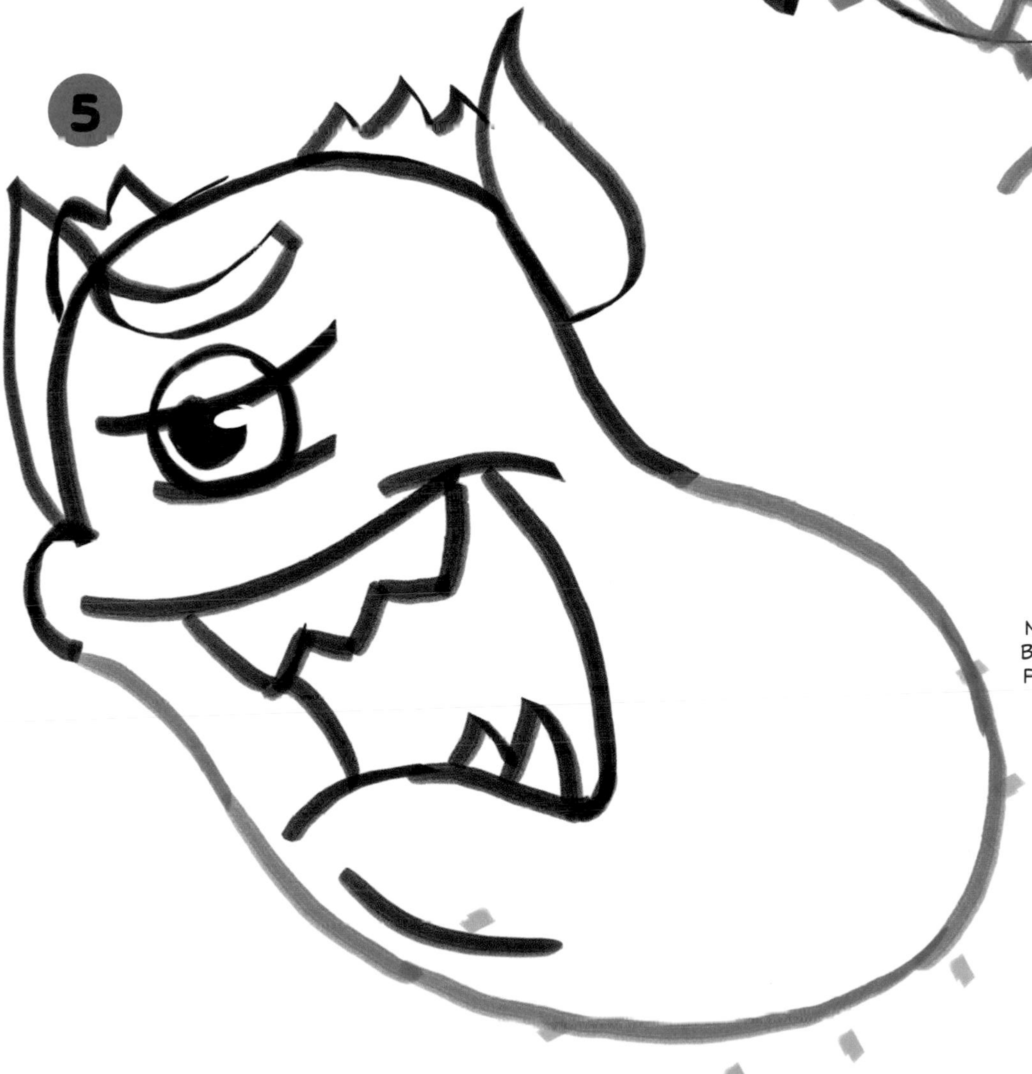

NOW THAT YOU KNOW HOW BIG THE MOUTH IS, YOU CAN FIT THE REST OF THE BODY AROUND IT.

WHEN PROVOKED, THE MONSCLARA MAKE THEMSELVES AS BIG AND THREATENING AS POSSIBLE. SKETCH THOSE BIG ARMS UP AND OUT FROM THE BODY.

6

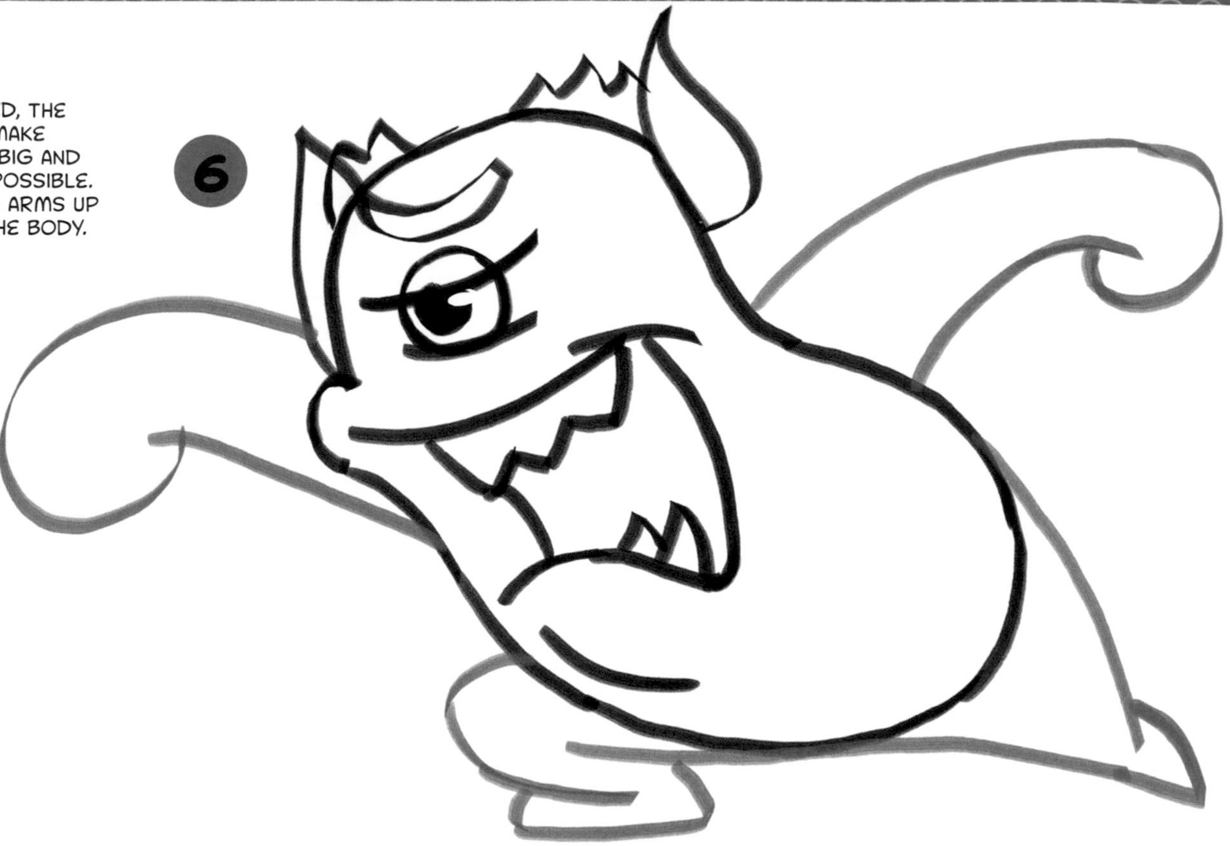

WHEN MAPPING OUT THE LOCATIONS FOR THE SPOTS, LOOK BACK AT THE STATIC POSE TO DRAW THEM IN THE SAME PLACES.

7

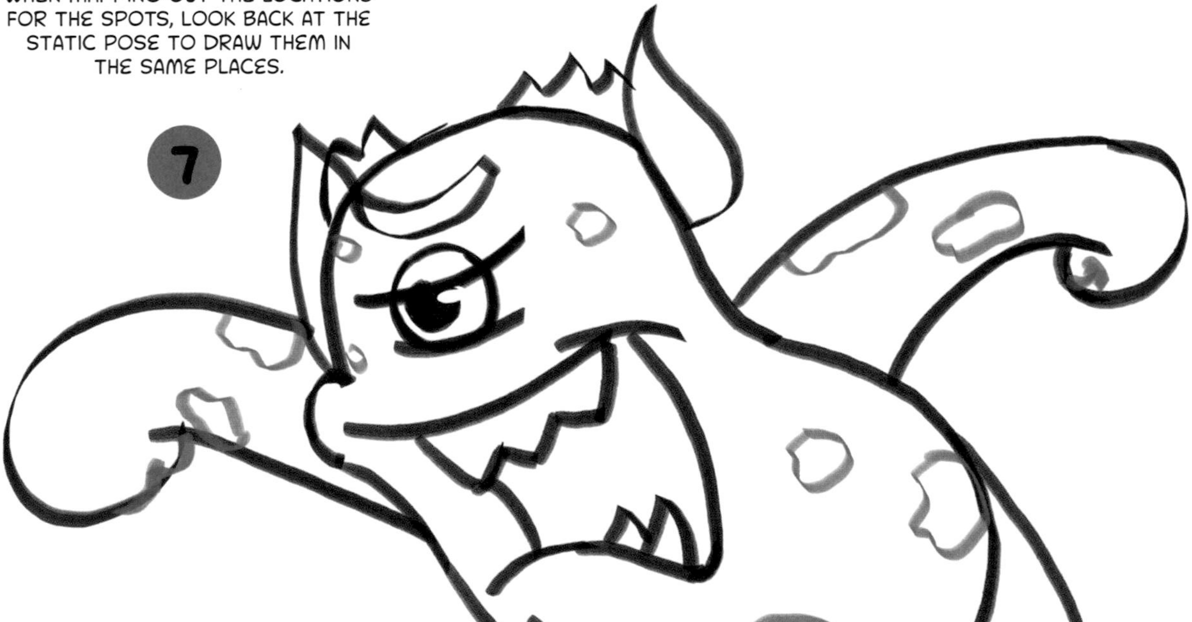

8

AFTER ADDING SOME COLOR TO YOUR CHARACTER, TRACE BACK AROUND SOME OF THE MAIN LINES AND MAKE THEM A LITTLE THICKER SO THE CHARACTER WILL POP OFF THE PAGE.

Make It Your Own!

Now let's change up the characters you just drew on pages 26 and 32 by altering the details. Here Tazu the Terror can become Steven Emperboa, and the Monsclara becomes a cold-weather Rauharr. You don't have to follow these exactly. Feel free to change the costumes, hair, facial expressions, or colors too!

1

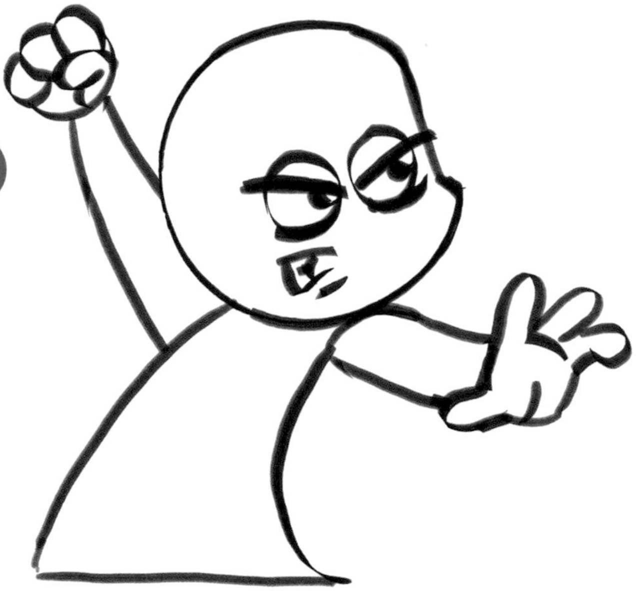

START WITH THE BASIC ACTION POSE FROM TAZU THE TERROR WITHOUT THE FACIAL HAIR AND ROBE DETAILS.

2

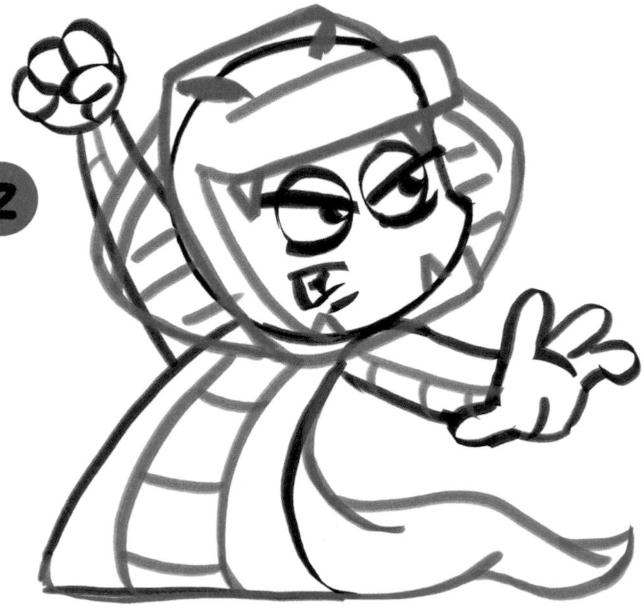

ADD TO THE TOP AND BACK OF THE ROBE TO MAKE THE CHARACTER'S BODY LONGER AND MORE SNAKELIKE.

3

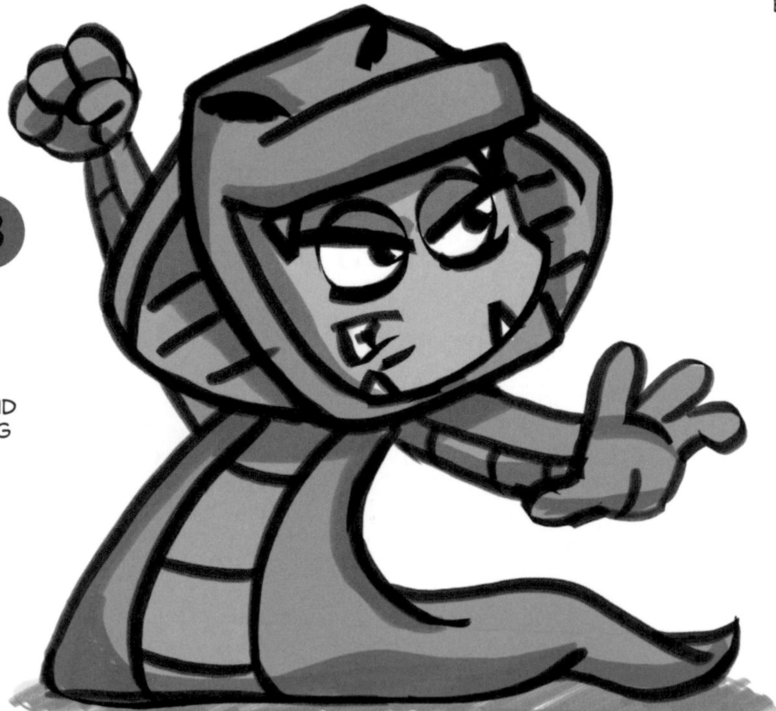

ERASE GUIDELINES AND ADD COLOR TO BRING THE WHOLE PIECE TOGETHER.

1 SKETCH OUT THE BASIC SHAPE OF THE MONSCLARA TO USE AS A TEMPLATE FOR A NEW MONSTER.

2 ADD WHATEVER YOU WANT TO MAKE IT YOUR OWN! HERE IS A CREATURE WITH ANTLERS, BONY SPIKES, AND A LOT OF FUR.

3 REMEMBER THAT WHEN EXPERIMENTING WITH CHARACTERS, YOU'RE FREE TO EXPERIMENT WITH COLORS TOO!

Battle Model KR-E2

Backstory: The KR series of mobile infantry Roi-bots are the latest creation from Roi Mechanical Industries. These units are designed for autonomous field operations with a strict obedience to their commanders. All of them except for KR-E2. After an electrical overload at the Roi factory, KR-E2 (or as they are now known KeRee) became fully sentient.

Motivation: KeRee wonder why they're different and if they can help other KRs wake up.

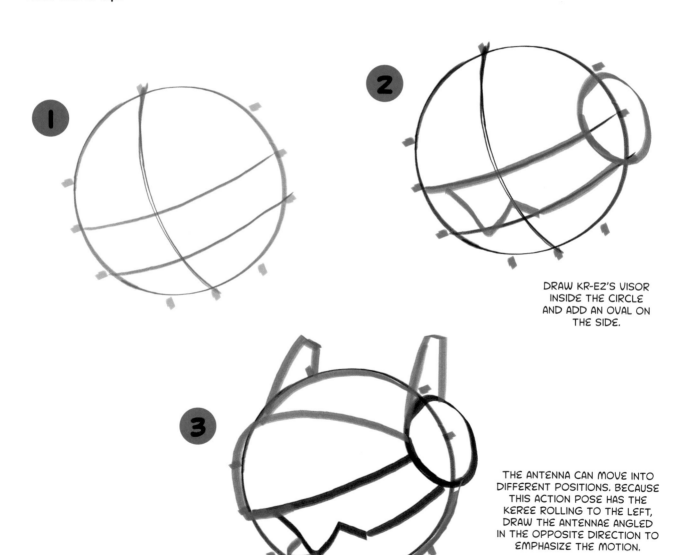

DRAW KR-E2'S VISOR
INSIDE THE CIRCLE
AND ADD AN OVAL ON
THE SIDE.

THE ANTENNA CAN MOVE INTO
DIFFERENT POSITIONS. BECAUSE
THIS ACTION POSE HAS THE
KEREE ROLLING TO THE LEFT,
DRAW THE ANTENNAE ANGLED
IN THE OPPOSITE DIRECTION TO
EMPHASIZE THE MOTION.

Powers: The KR series is highly adaptable to their situations.
Limitations: The KR series is a bit of an energy hog and is in constant need of recharging.

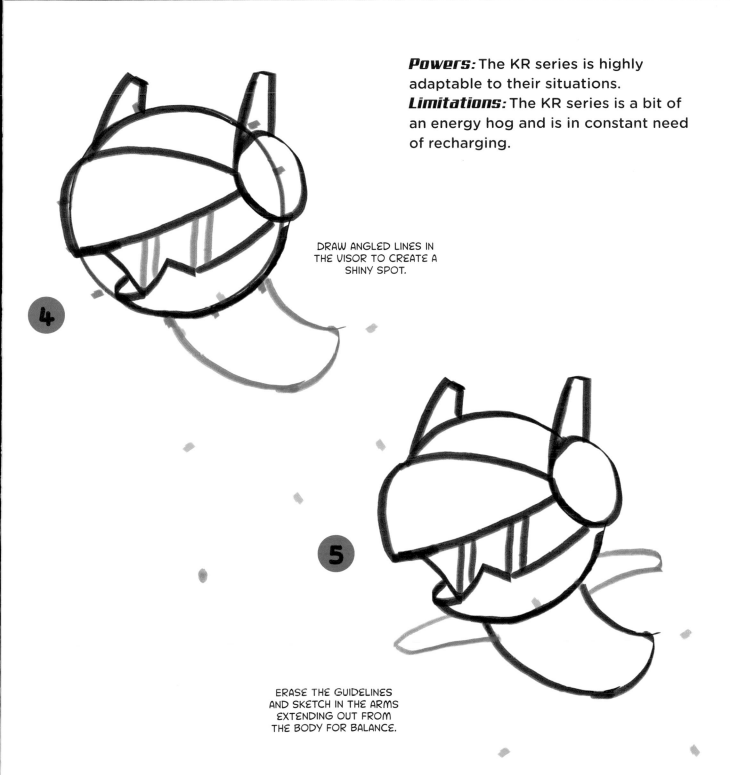

DRAW ANGLED LINES IN THE VISOR TO CREATE A SHINY SPOT.

ERASE THE GUIDELINES AND SKETCH IN THE ARMS EXTENDING OUT FROM THE BODY FOR BALANCE.

Backstory: Kaoh's impulsive nature ended up getting him into trouble on more than one occasion. While training for a pepper-eating contest, Kaoh mistook his roommate's science experiment for a hot pepper, resulting in his newfound ability.

Motivation: Kaoh is seeking his center, his happy place. He hopes to find it by helping others, but he feels that his new powers mean that he will never quite fit in.

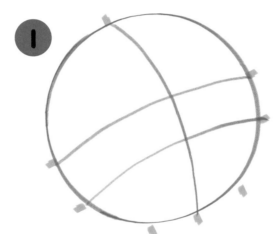

ANGLE YOUR VERTICAL AND HORIZONTAL GUIDELINES SO THAT KAOH WILL BE LOOKING UPWARD.

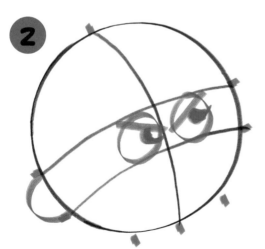

AFTER DRAWING THE CIRCLES FOR THE EYES, ADD DIAGONAL LINES TO THEM TO MAKE THEM MORE INTENSE.

HAVING THE EYEBROWS FORMING A "V" SHAPE WILL ADD TO THE INTENSE EXPRESSION.

Powers: Kaoh has the ability to control the fire that has engulfed his body. With it he has flight power and fireball blasters.

Limitations: He can't completely turn off his flame powers. Through forced meditation he can appear to be almost normal, but there's always a warm glow around him.

ERASE YOUR GUIDELINES BEFORE MEASURING THE BODY HEIGHT, WHICH IS THE SAME HEIGHT AS THE HEAD CIRCLE. START WITH AN ANGLED BOX FOR THE CHEST AND SIMPLE SHAPES FOR THE HANDS AND ARMS.

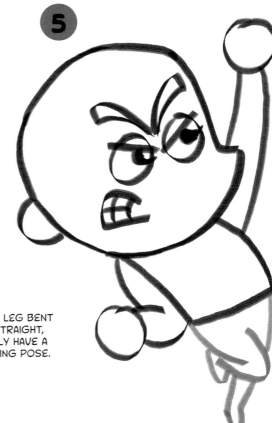

BY DRAWING ONE LEG BENT AND ONE LEG STRAIGHT, YOU IMMEDIATELY HAVE A JUMPING OR FLYING POSE.

Drake

Backstory: Drake loves the phrase, "You can't judge a book by its cover." You see, this little guy is a Gargan and has the ability to change his appearance. He was lost in space after an asteroid storm damaged his ship.
Motivation: Drake is all about looking out for the little guy and is a bold defender of fair treatment for all.

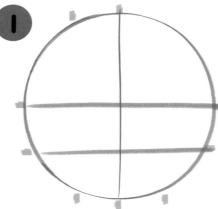

LINE UP DRAKE'S EYES AND EARS BETWEEN THE HORIZONTAL GUIDELINES.

DRAKE MAY BE SMALL, BUT HE'S GOT BIG HAIR! THIS TIME THE BODY IS ABOUT HALF THE HEIGHT OF THE HEAD CIRCLE.

Powers: Drake is a morphling and can change into limitless shapes and forms.
Limitations: The longer he stays in another form, the more energy he loses. He can't hold his transformations indefinitely.

ADD SIMPLE CIRCLES AT THE HIPS FOR THE HANDS, AND THEN CONNECT THOSE CIRCLES TO THE HEAD WITH AN ANGLED LINE.

AFTER ADDING SOME DETAILS TO THE OUTFIT, ADD COLOR.

Make It Your Own!

Now let's change up the characters on pages 44 and 48 by altering the details. With a few changes, you can make Kaoh and Drake become totally new characters. You don't have to follow these drawings exactly. Feel free to change the costumes, hair, facial expressions, or colors.

1

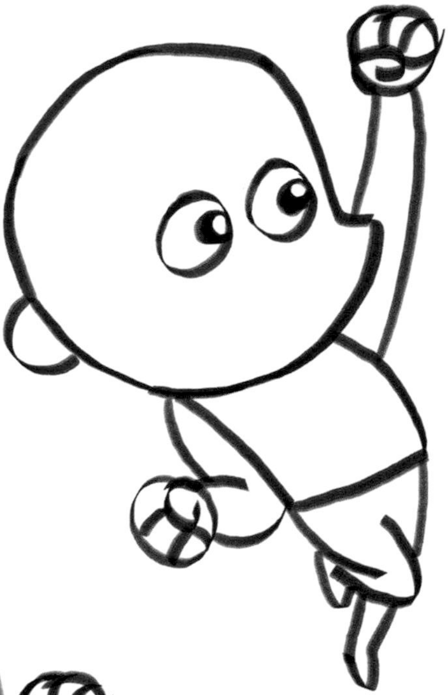

KAOH'S ACTION POSE IS PERFECT FOR OTHER FLYING CHARACTERS.

2

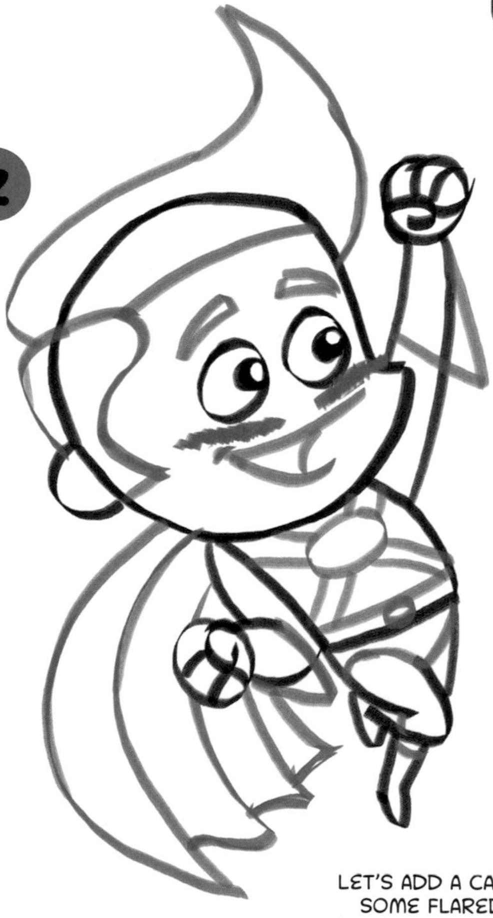

LET'S ADD A CAPE, SOME FLARED GLOVES, AND SOME SUPER STYLISH HAIR!

3

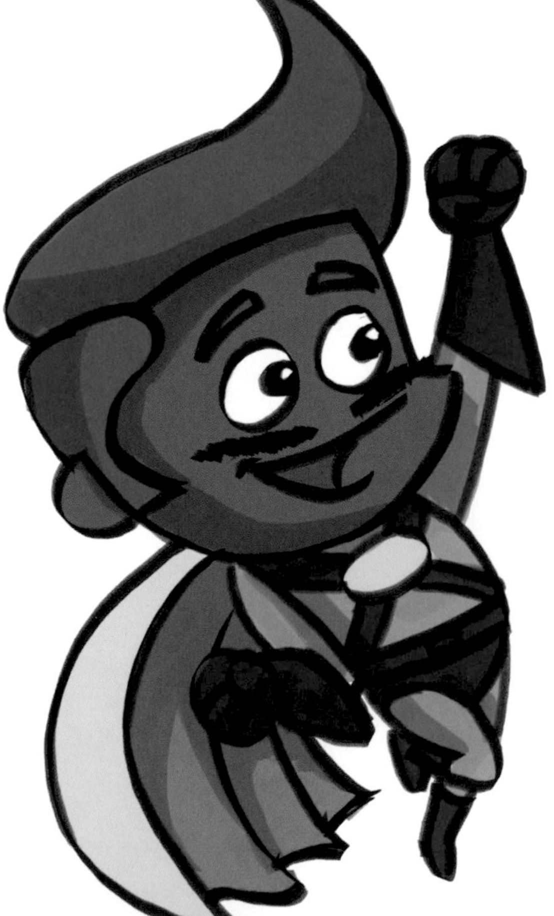

START WITH DRAKE'S STANDING POSE.

1

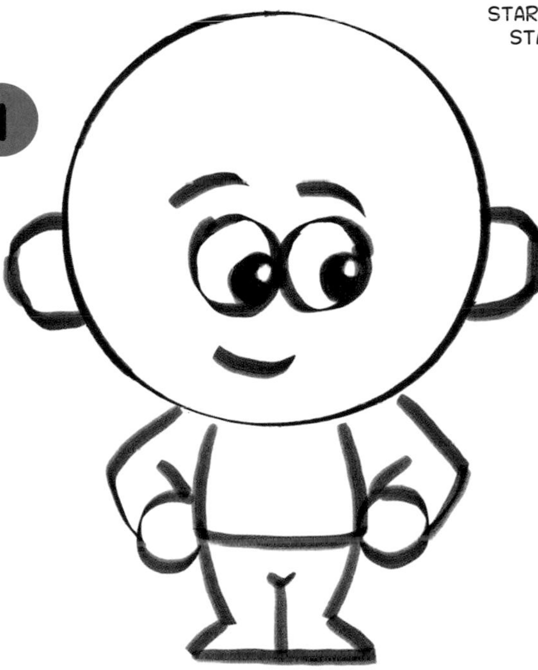

2

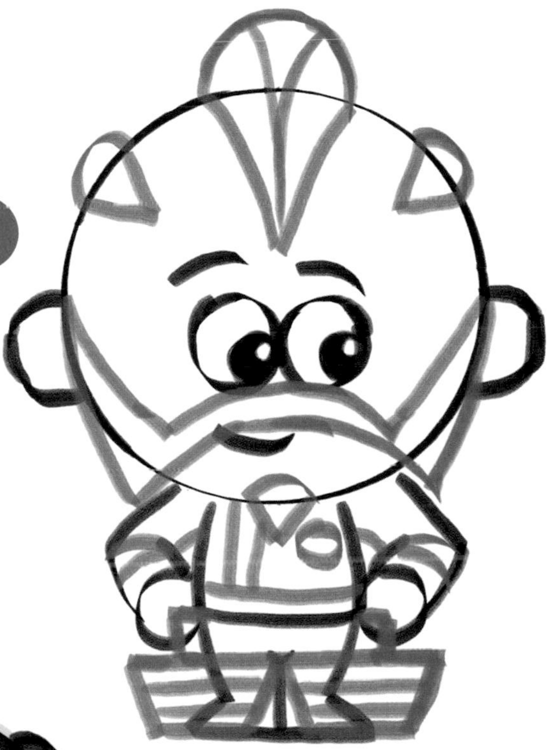

REPLACE THE LEGS WITH ROLLING TREADS AND DRAW AN AWESOME MUSTACHE!

3

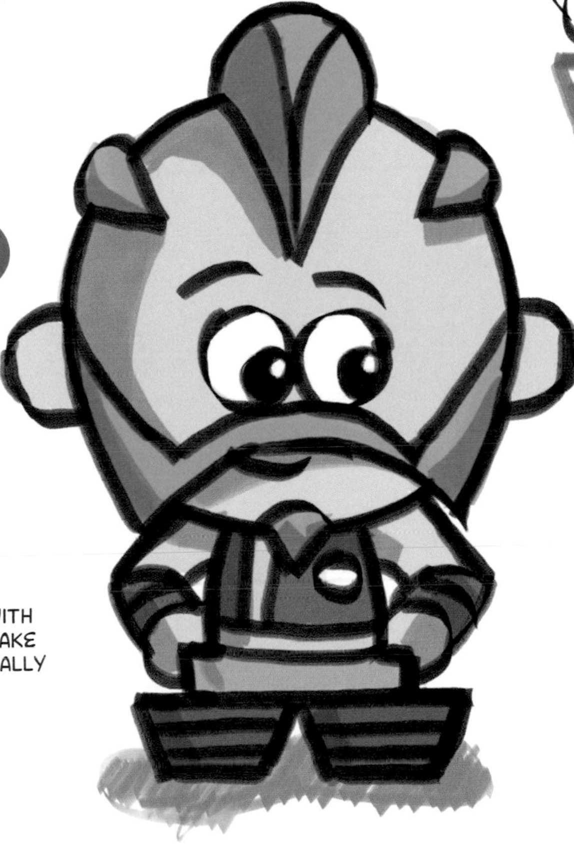

HAVE SOME FUN WITH THE COLOR AND MAKE THAT MUSTACHE REALLY STAND OUT!

Developing a Story

Simply put, all stories have a beginning (first act), middle (second act), and an end (third act). Before you start drawing a comic book, first write a script of what's going to happen in the story. While telling the story, remember that the absence of information will better draw in your audience. Instead of saying everything up front, let your characters' backstories, goals, motivations, powers, and limitations reveal themselves slowly through their actions.

First Act

In the beginning, all is well, and life is normal. Then something happens; there is conflict. There is an unknown element introduced that challenges your hero. The first act ends when the hero decides to take action against the unknown element, and that decision sets the tone for the next act.

**First Act:
Departure**

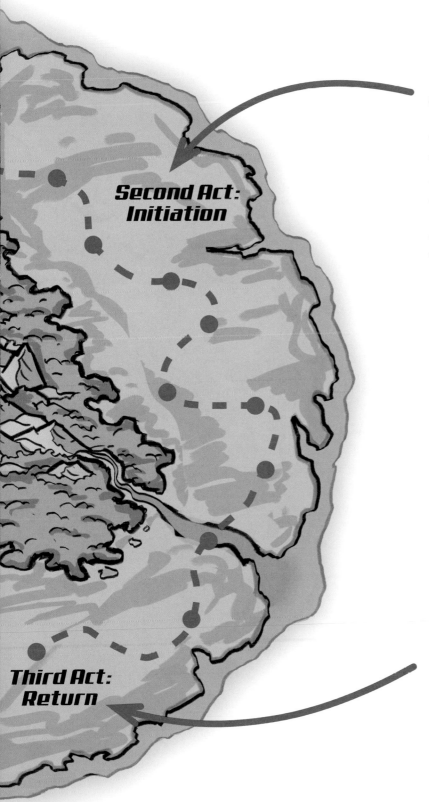

Second Act

In the middle of the story, the hero faces the first of many obstacles, tests the limits of his or her powers, and begins to understand the challenges ahead. The audience learns more about the motivations of the villain and sees the hero tested. This act ends with the hero facing the most difficult challenge of all.

Second Act: Initiation

Third Act: Return

Third Act

The end of the story sees the transformed hero return to normal life—with a new perspective and ready for the next adventure.

Alleyne

Backstory: Alleyne is the smallest person on a planet full of giants. She's always felt a little out-of-place and signed up for an exchange program with a neighboring planet but was zapped through a warp tunnel and accidentally ended up on Earth.

Motivation: Alleyne knows what it feels like to be a bit of an outsider and wants to help others find their own worth.

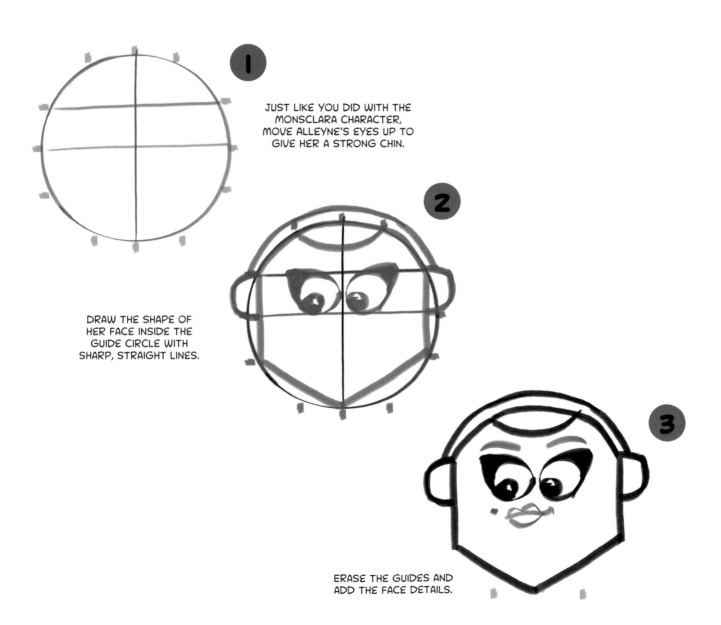

1

JUST LIKE YOU DID WITH THE MONSCLARA CHARACTER, MOVE ALLEYNE'S EYES UP TO GIVE HER A STRONG CHIN.

2

DRAW THE SHAPE OF HER FACE INSIDE THE GUIDE CIRCLE WITH SHARP, STRAIGHT LINES.

3

ERASE THE GUIDES AND ADD THE FACE DETAILS.

Powers: Being from a completely different world, Alleyne's body is incredibly dense and strong. Along with that strength, Earth's gravity has less of an affect on her, and she is able to jump vast distances.
Limitations: All of the differences that come from being on a new planet take some getting used to. Alleyne doesn't have complete control of these newfound powers and finds herself stumbling through her day.

BECAUSE ALLEYNE IS SO TALL, HER TORSO IS THE SAME HEIGHT AS THE HEAD CIRCLE.

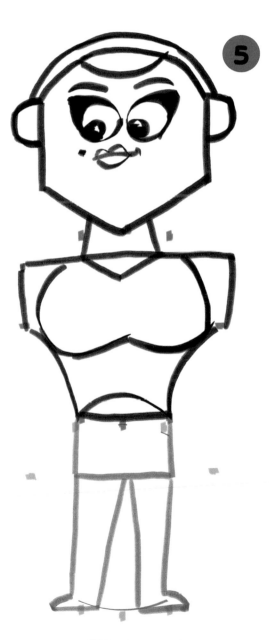

THE HEIGHT OF HER LEGS IS ALSO THE SAME HEIGHT AS THE HEAD CIRCLE.

6

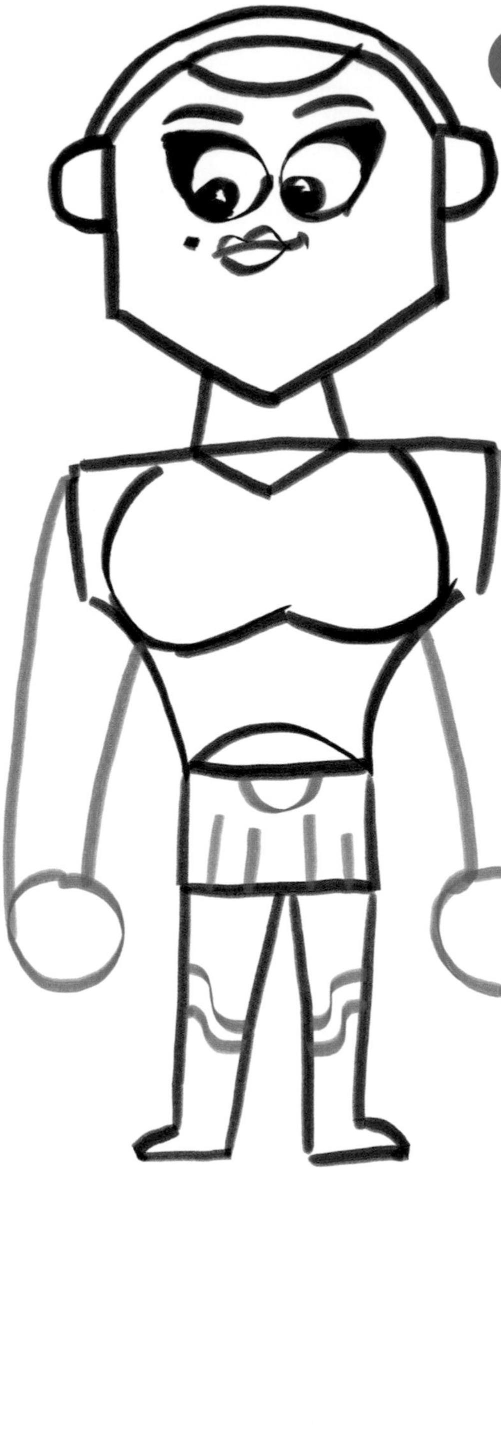

DRAW ALLEYNE'S LONG, STRONG ARMS BY DRAWING CIRCLES FOR THE HANDS NEAR THE LEGS AND CONNECTING THE HANDS TO HER SHOULDERS.

7

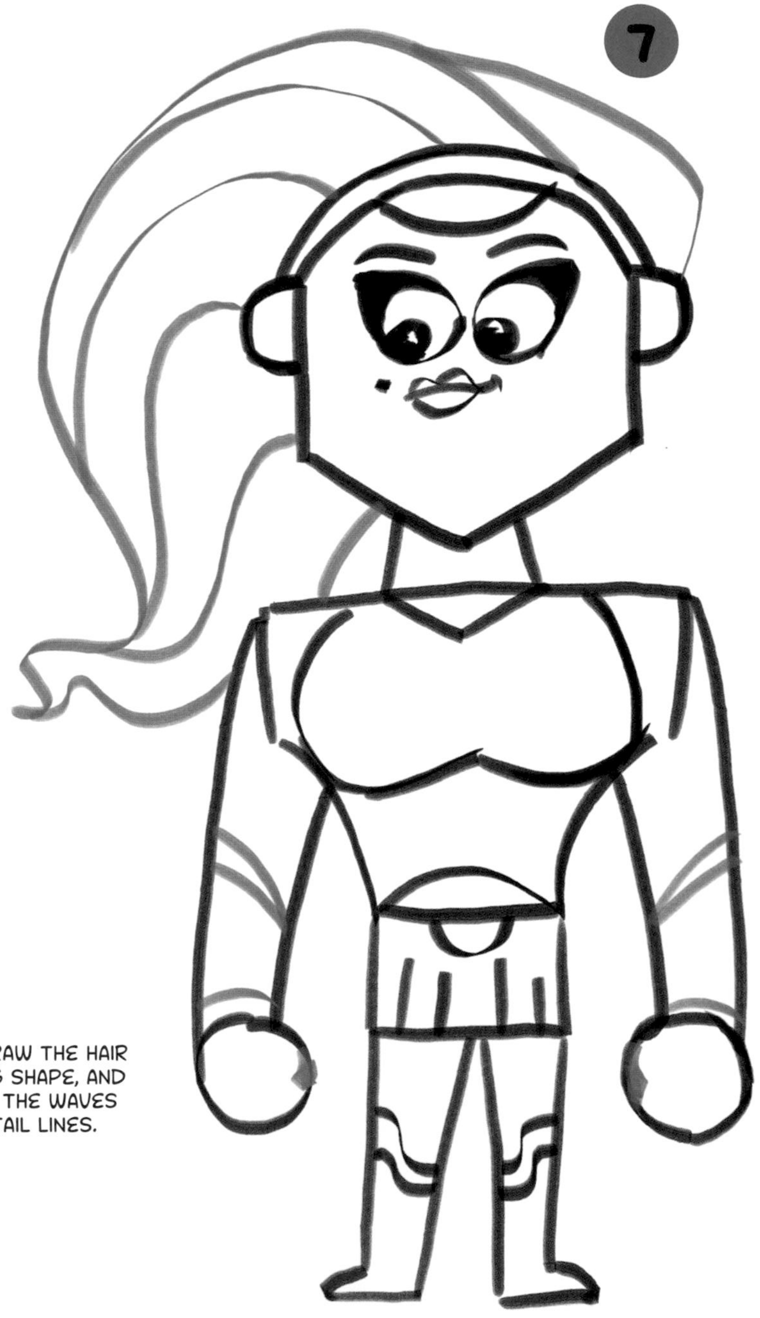

LIGHTLY DRAW THE HAIR AS ONE BIG SHAPE, AND THEN ADD THE WAVES AND DETAIL LINES.

YOU DON'T HAVE TO GO
CRAZY WITH DETAILS TO
SHADE YOUR CHARACTER.
TO CREATE A FEELING OF
DEPTH, ADD SOME DARKER
COLORS TO THE SIDE OF
THE FACE AND CHIN, AND ON
THE INSIDES OF THE ARMS.

Kenzee

Backstory: The sole survivor of a shipwreck, Kenzee woke on an island beach with no memory of his past. It wasn't until he was rescued that he discovered that his blue skin and green hair were an anomaly.
Motivation: Kenzee is driven to uncover his past as a way to understand his place in the world.
Powers: During the time that Kenzee was stranded on the island, he learned to control water, as well as the moisture in the air. He can use this power to lift objects and even fly.
Limitations: Kenzee must avoid heat and dehydration at all costs.

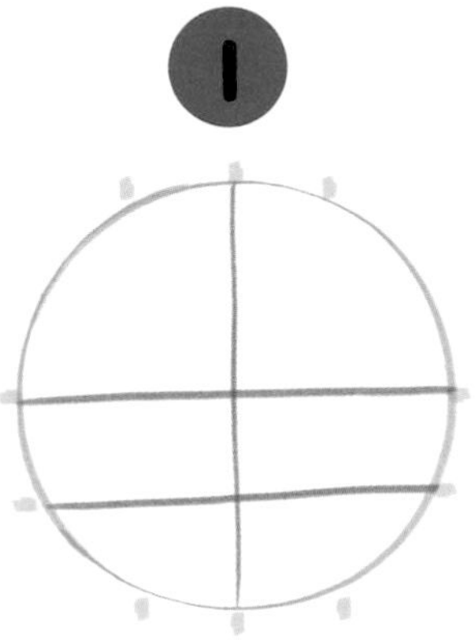
1

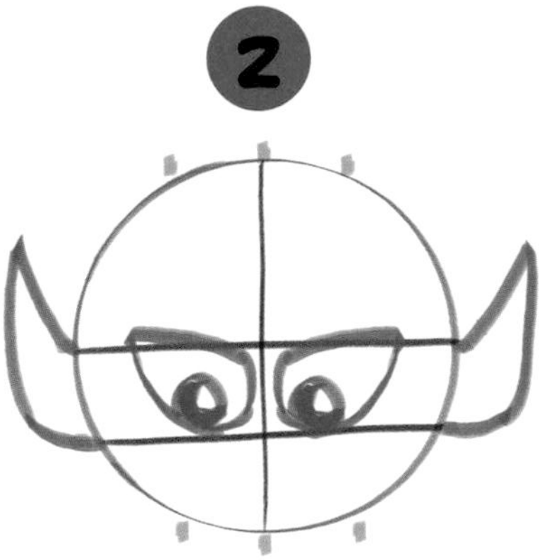
2

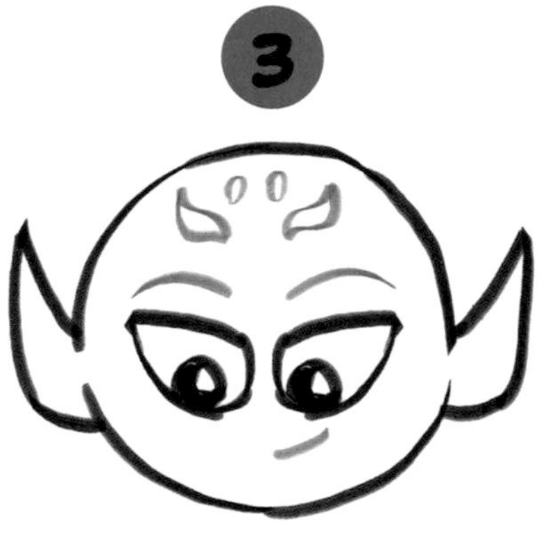
3

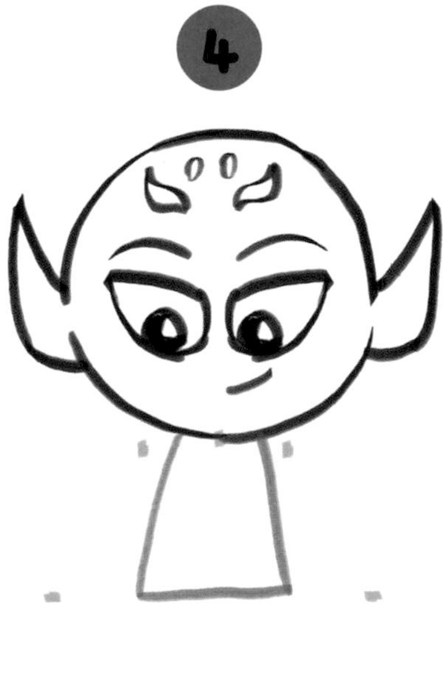
4

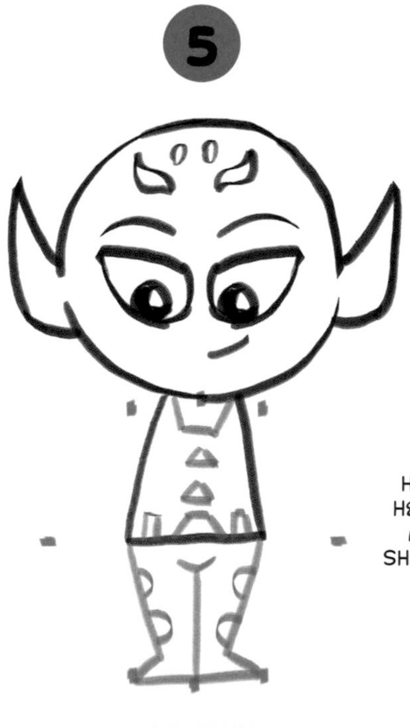
5

THE WAISTLINE IS HALFWAY DOWN THE HEIGHT OF THE BODY. ADD SMALL DETAIL SHAPES TO THE TORSO AND THE LEGS.

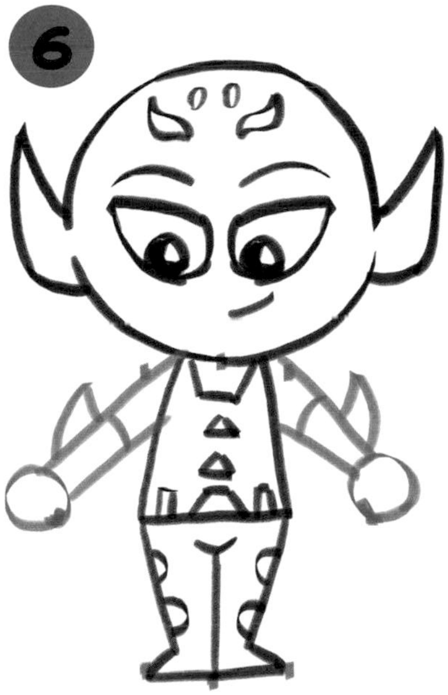

ANGLING THE ARMS AWAY FROM THE BODY WILL ADD TO THE SENSE THAT KENZEE IS GETTING READY TO USE HIS POWERS.

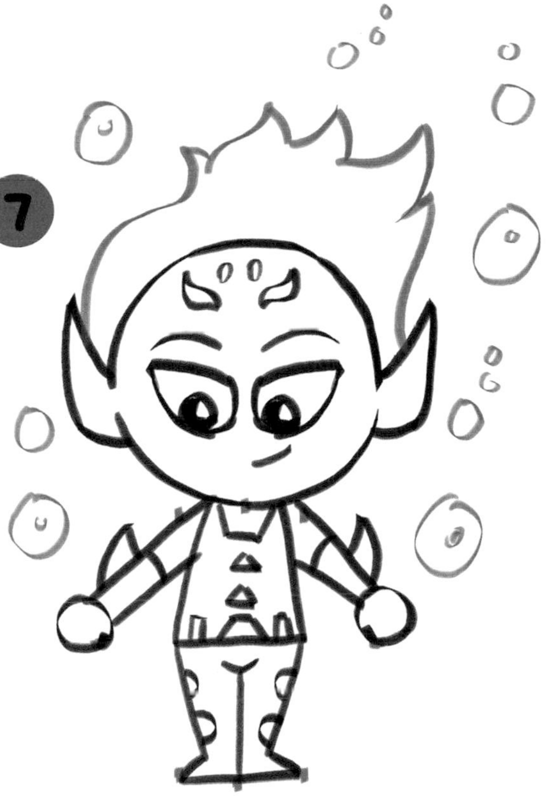

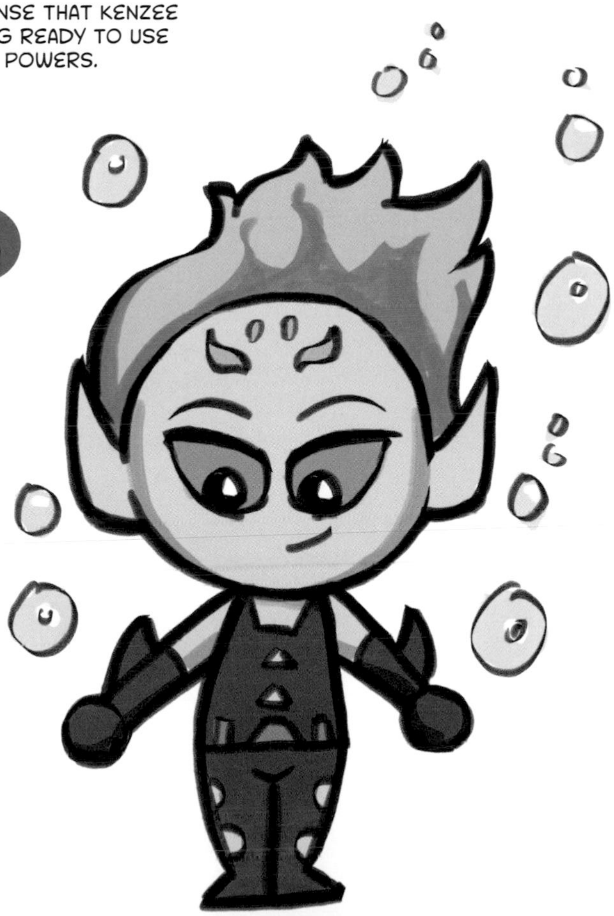

DRAW THE HAIR UP AND AWAY FROM THE HEAD TO MAKE IT LOOK LIKE IT'S FLOATING. ADD WATER BUBBLES OF DIFFERENT SIZES AND SHAPES AROUND KENZEE.

Dr. Darkness

Backstory: Kiren Long was working to discover the mysterious properties of "dark matter" when an accident in the lab exposed her to the sample she was working with.
Motivation: The dark matter seems to have polarized Dr. Darkness' sense of right and wrong. She seeks to put the world into a perfect balance.

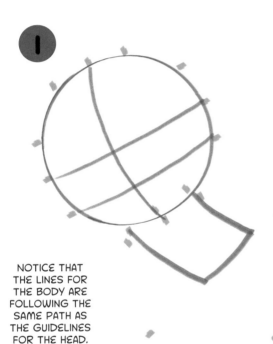

1

NOTICE THAT THE LINES FOR THE BODY ARE FOLLOWING THE SAME PATH AS THE GUIDELINES FOR THE HEAD.

2

CONTINUE THE LOWER BODY LINE TO CREATE THE LINE FOR THE LEG. THIS CONTINUOUS SHAPE CREATES A FLUID LINE OF ACTION.

3

DRAW THE ARMS AND ADD THE DETAILS TO THE HAT AND COAT.

Powers: Dr. Darkness moves like a shadow and uses the dark to heighten a person's fear of the unknown.
Limitations: Dr. Darkness is limited by the light. She only has powers in the dark.

4

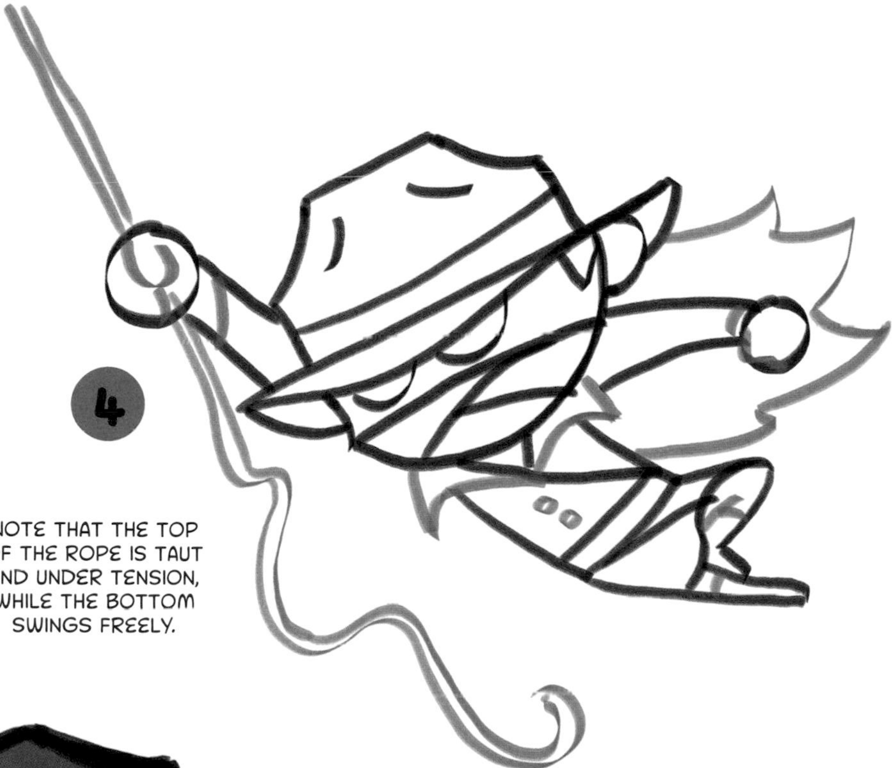

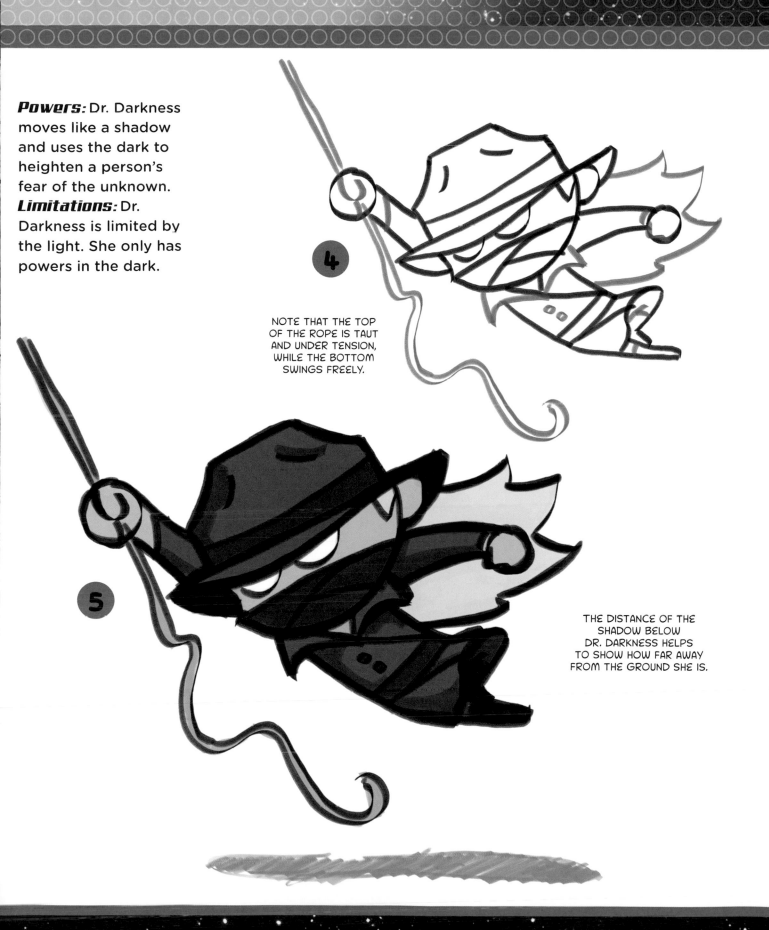

NOTE THAT THE TOP OF THE ROPE IS TAUT AND UNDER TENSION, WHILE THE BOTTOM SWINGS FREELY.

5

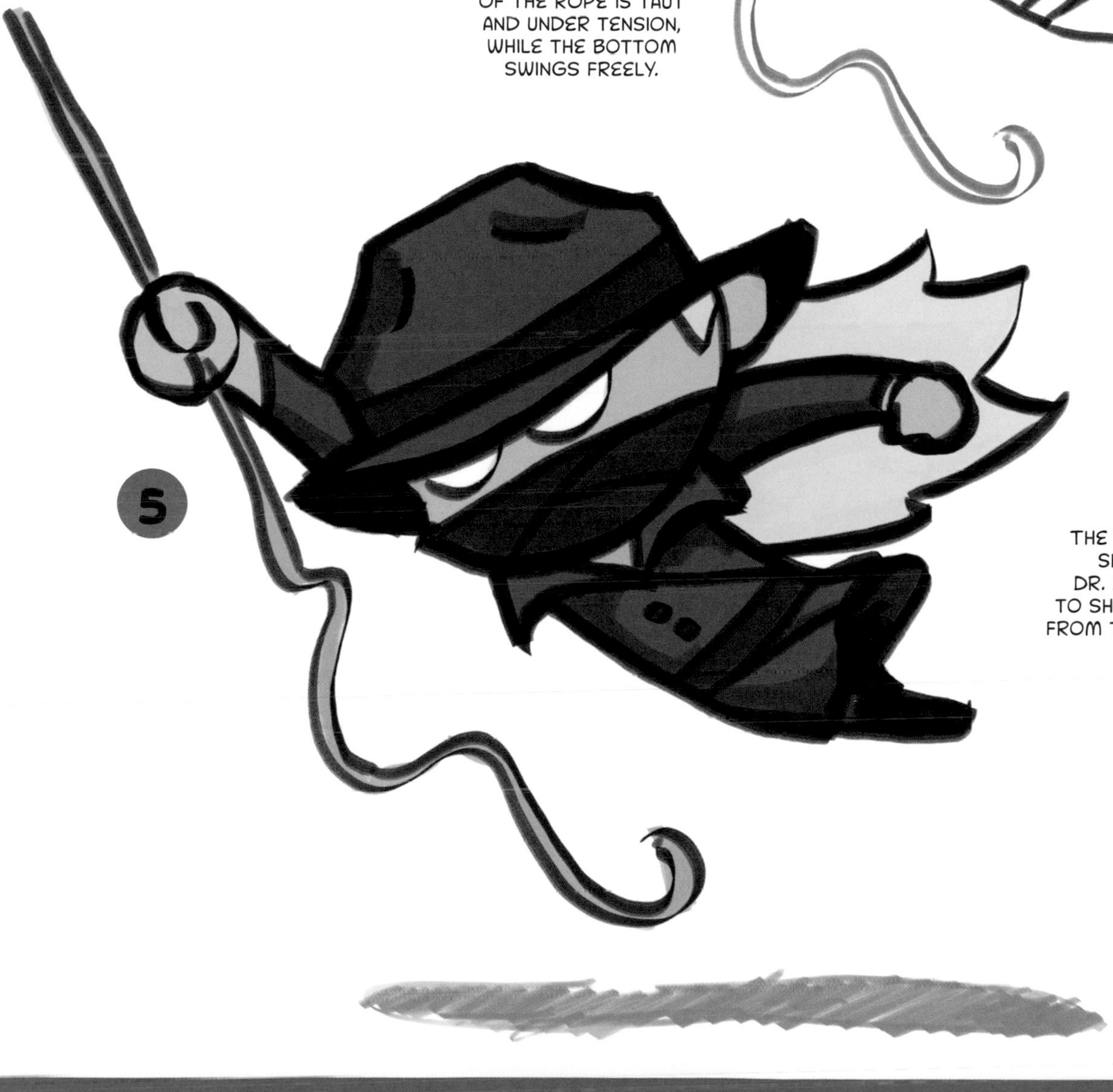

THE DISTANCE OF THE SHADOW BELOW DR. DARKNESS HELPS TO SHOW HOW FAR AWAY FROM THE GROUND SHE IS.

Make It Your Own!

Now let's change up Kenzee (page 58) and Dr. Darkness (page 60) by altering their details. And remember, you don't have to follow these example drawings exactly. After you've drawn your characters, think about what they are like. What could their names be? What are their backstories and motivations, their powers and limitations?

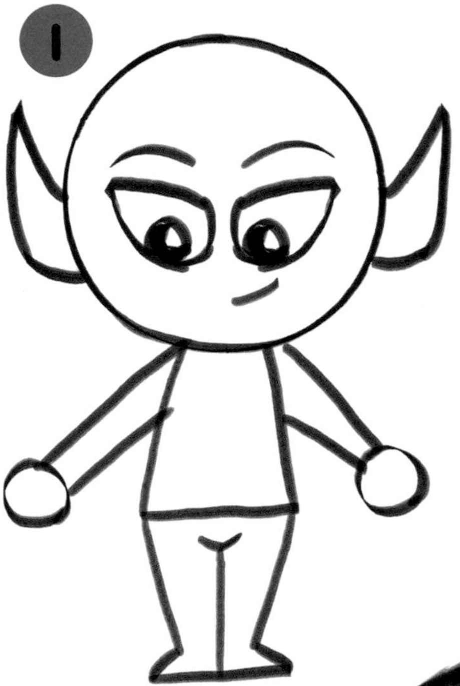

KENZEE HAS AN ALIEN LOOK TO HIM. LET'S USE HIS STANDING POSE TO MAKE A DIFFERENT ALIEN.

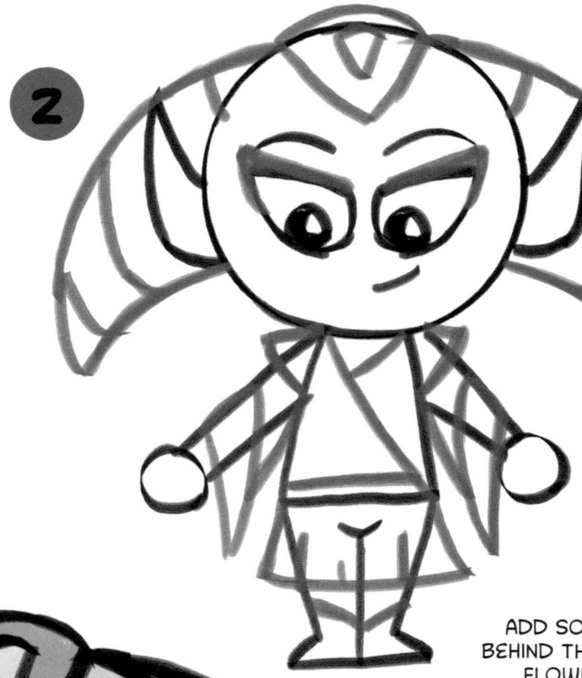

ADD SOME SHAPES BEHIND THE HEAD AND A FLOWING ROBE.

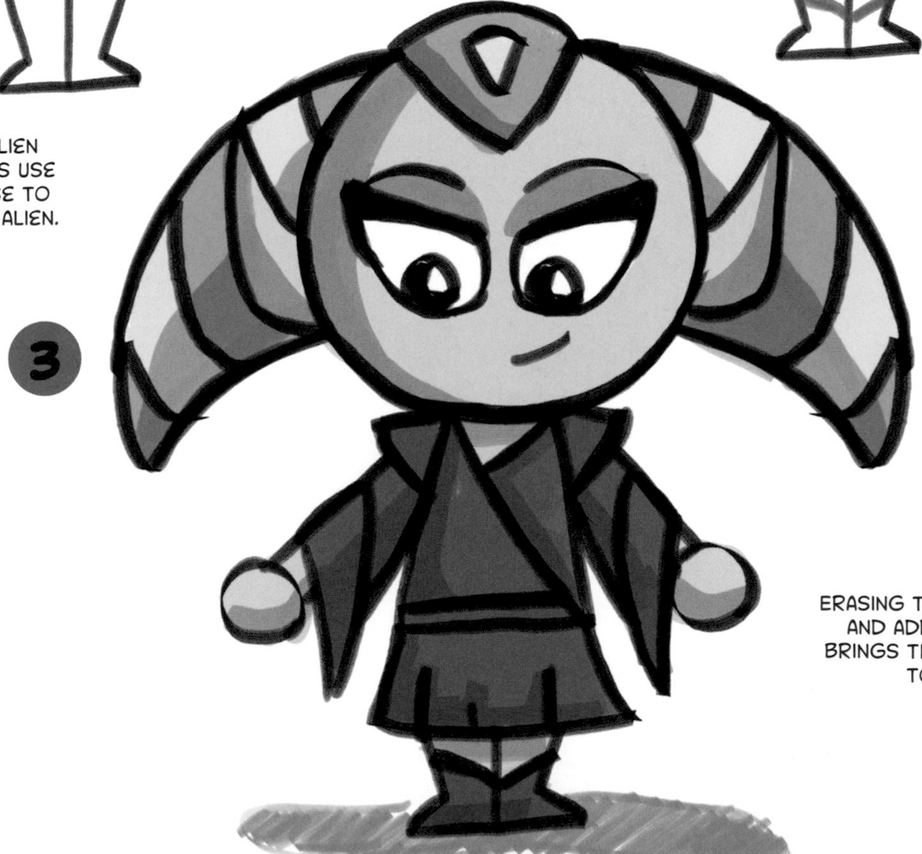

ERASING THE GUIDELINES AND ADDING COLOR BRINGS THE CHARACTER TO LIFE.

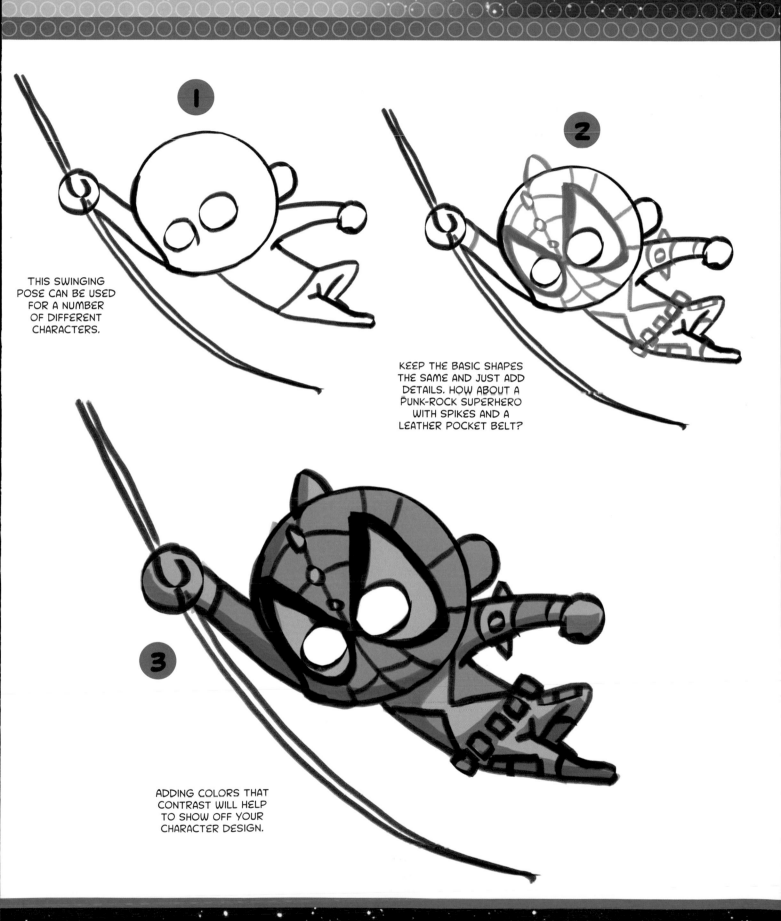

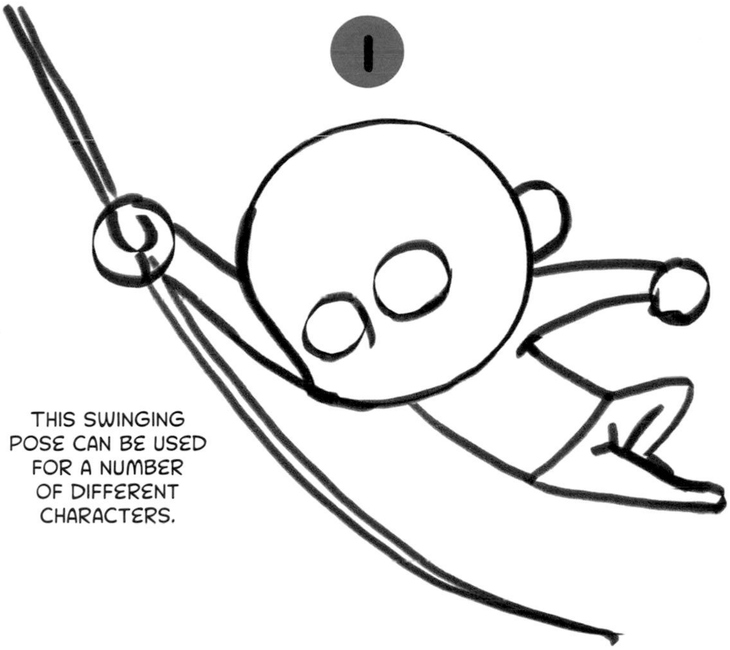
1

THIS SWINGING POSE CAN BE USED FOR A NUMBER OF DIFFERENT CHARACTERS.

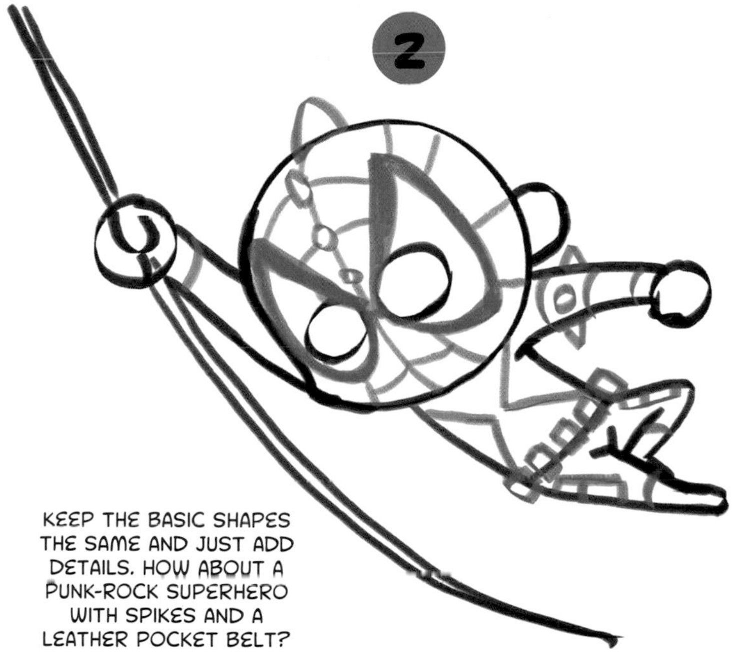
2

KEEP THE BASIC SHAPES THE SAME AND JUST ADD DETAILS. HOW ABOUT A PUNK-ROCK SUPERHERO WITH SPIKES AND A LEATHER POCKET BELT?

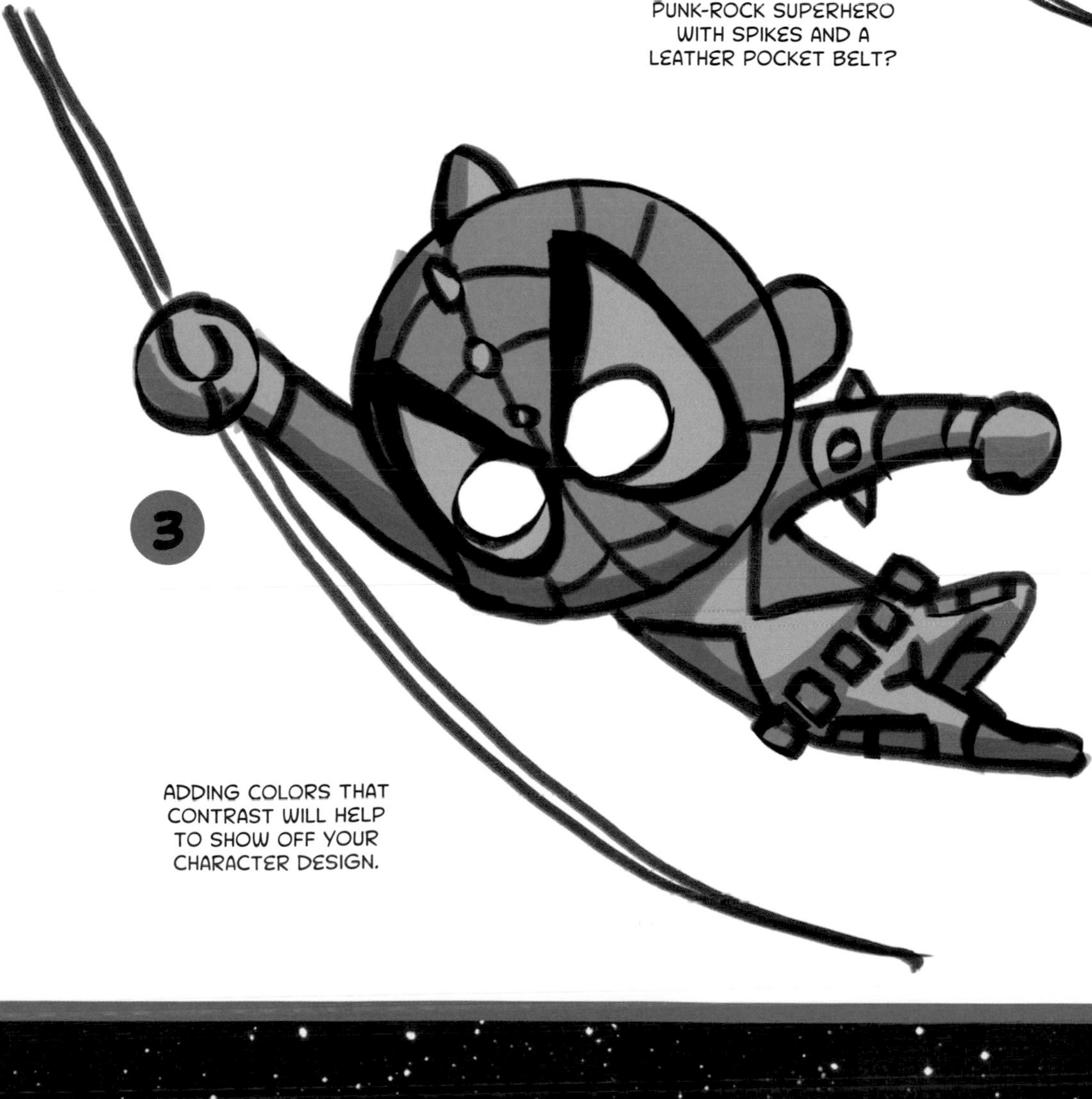
3

ADDING COLORS THAT CONTRAST WILL HELP TO SHOW OFF YOUR CHARACTER DESIGN.

Using Panels

There's more to comic book panels than simply dividing up your page into smaller boxes. The size, shape, and direction of the panels will help tell your story.

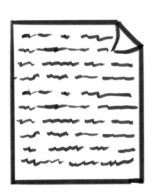

Start your comic book by writing out a loose script based on your story (see pages 52-53).

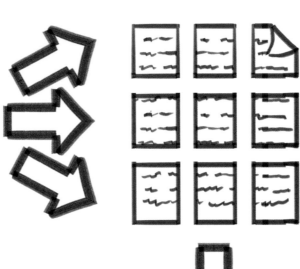

Plan how the script will flow onto each page of your comic book. Planning your pages ahead of time will ensure that you are including something interesting on each page. Look for a way to tell a complete piece of the story on each page, and when possible, try to end each page with some sort of mystery. This will encourage your reader to keep reading and discover what comes next.

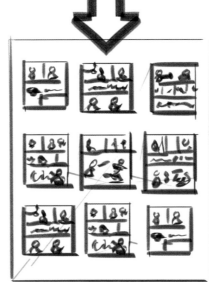

Create a rough sketch outline for all of the pages in the story. These thumbnail sketches will help you get a better understanding of where to put all your panels.

The first panel should establish the location and mood. Refer back to your script. Are your characters in the city or the jungle? Maybe they're floating out in the vacuum of space. This can be a very large panel on the page.

As your story continues, add variation to the sizes of the panels and even the sizes of the characters in the panel.

As you continue through your script, remember that your story drives your panels.

As a general rule, don't make more than nine panels for each page. If you have more boxes than that, it can be a strain on the eyes.

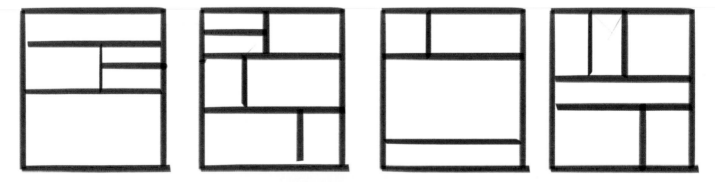

Spelk

Backstory: The long-legged Spelk use their green coloring to camouflage themselves in the deep woods. It is in these woods that they live incredibly long and quiet lives.

Motivation: Spelk want nothing more than to be left alone. Any interruption to their serene lifestyle is met with extreme fear. They'll do just about anything to get back to a calm and quiet life.

Powers: Spelk can climb just about anything and blend in with their surroundings.

Limitations: Spelk are unusually afraid of everything.

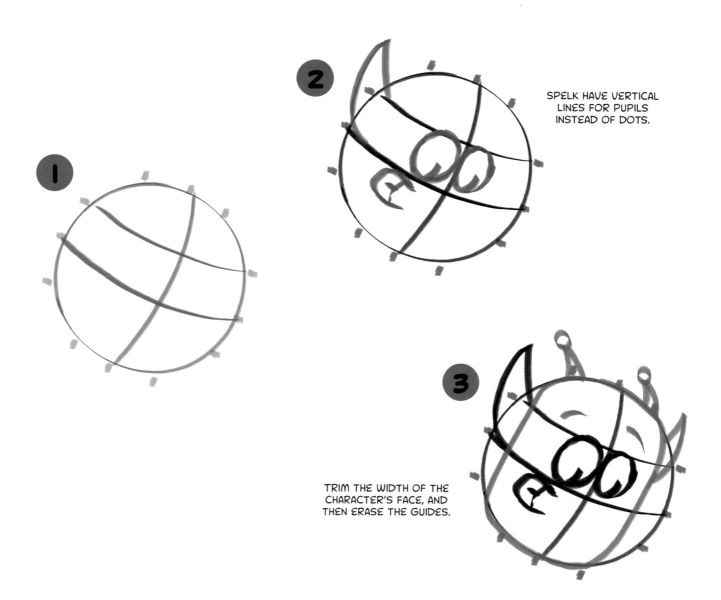

SPELK HAVE VERTICAL LINES FOR PUPILS INSTEAD OF DOTS.

TRIM THE WIDTH OF THE CHARACTER'S FACE, AND THEN ERASE THE GUIDES.

4 DRAW A SMALL SQUARE UNDER THE HEAD FOR THE SMALL BODY AND A VERTICAL LINE FOR THE WALL WITH A SET OF FEET ON IT.

5 CONNECT THE FEET TO BODY TO CREATE THE SPELK'S LONG LEGS.

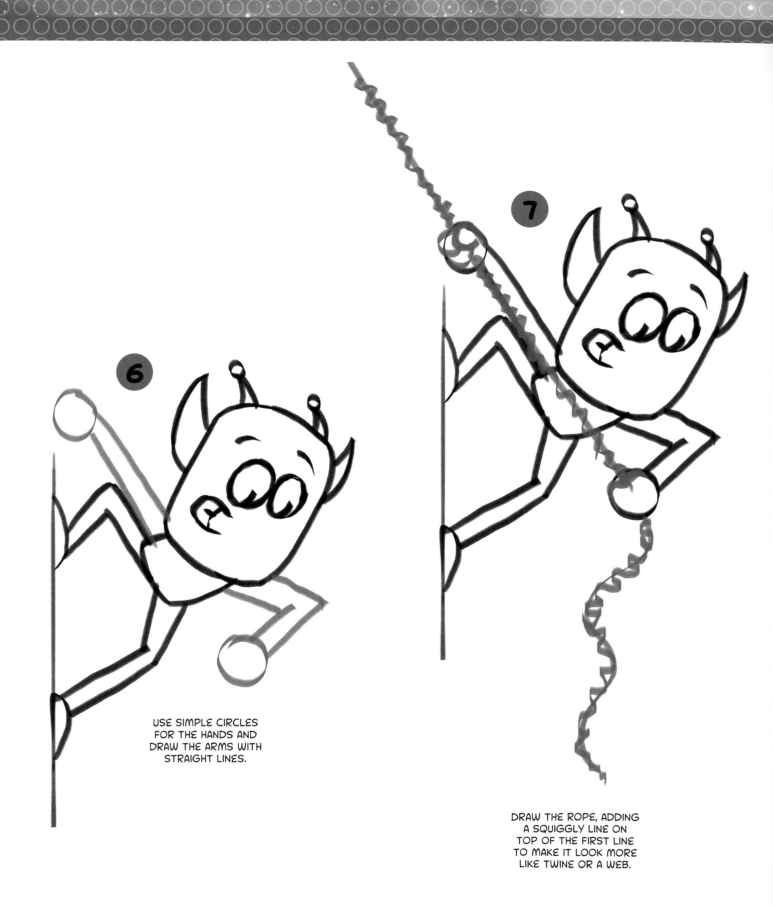

6

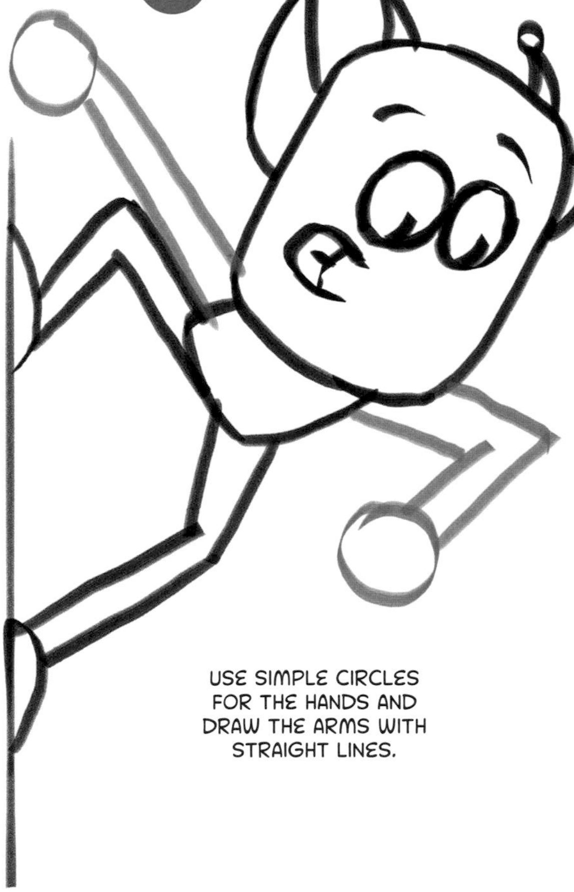

USE SIMPLE CIRCLES
FOR THE HANDS AND
DRAW THE ARMS WITH
STRAIGHT LINES.

7

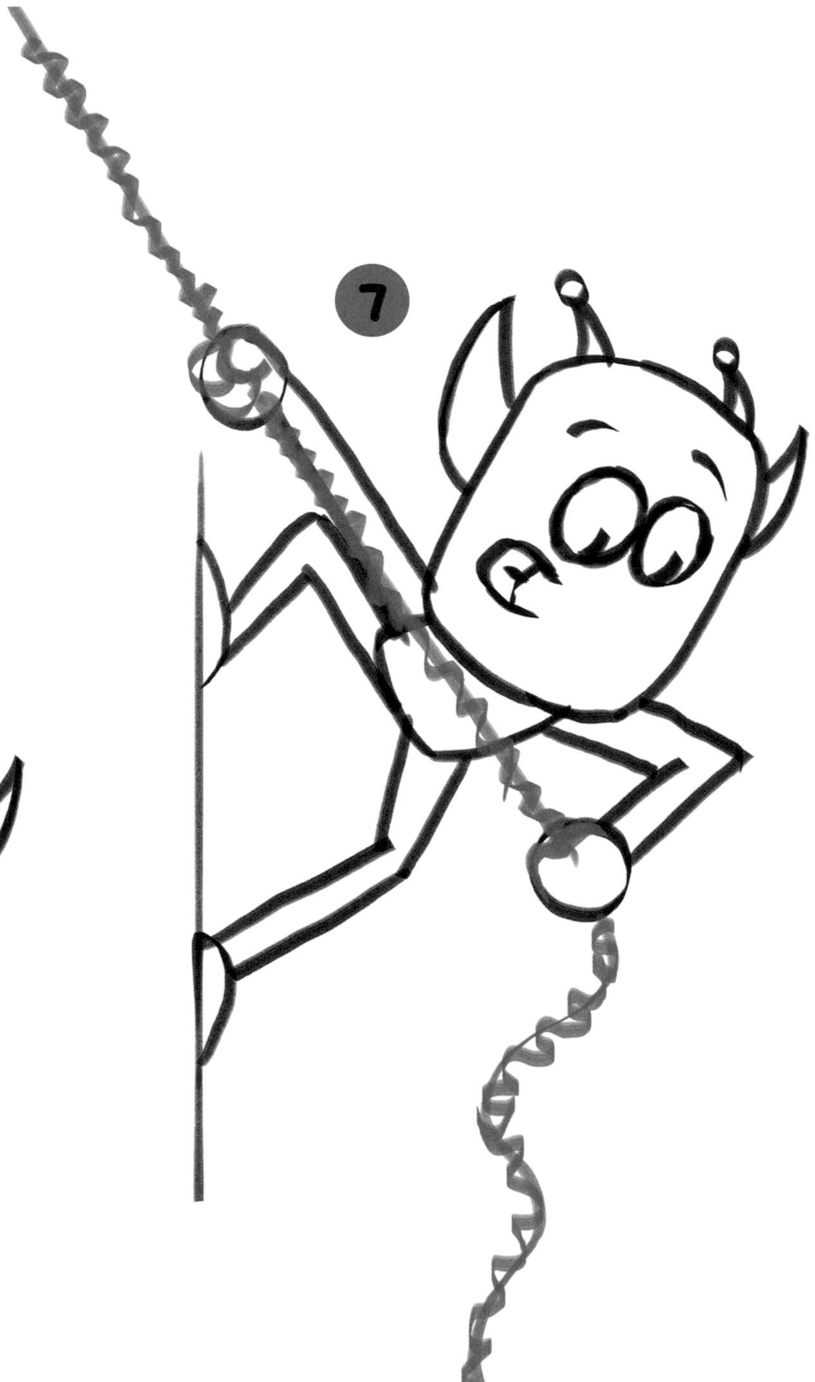

DRAW THE ROPE, ADDING
A SQUIGGLY LINE ON
TOP OF THE FIRST LINE
TO MAKE IT LOOK MORE
LIKE TWINE OR A WEB.

A Spelk's natural ability to climb pales in comparison to its ability to run away from dangerous situations. This particular retreating Spelk is demonstrating the "Flail and Flee" technique first made famous by Sirobin the Brave.

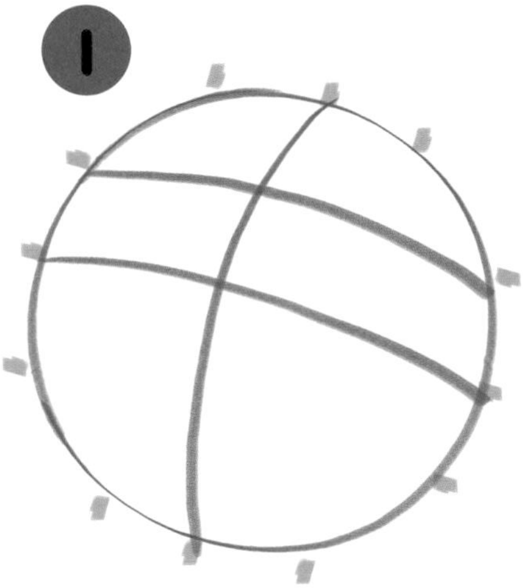

BECAUSE THIS SPELK IS SCARED, ITS PUPILS ARE SMALL DOTS INSTEAD OF A VERTICAL LINE.

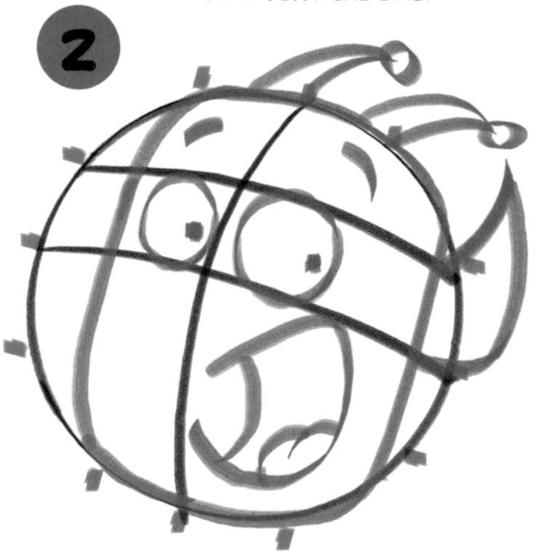

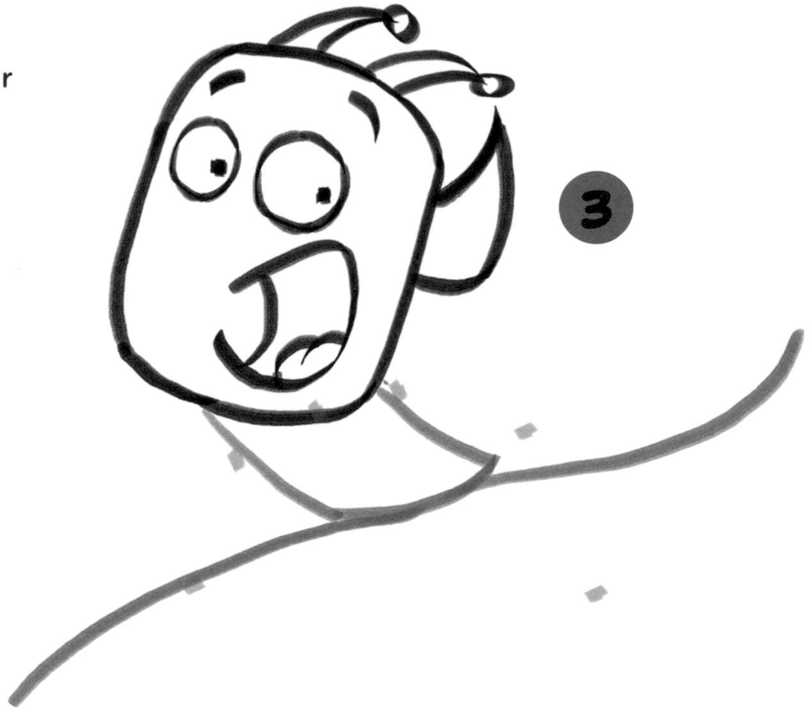

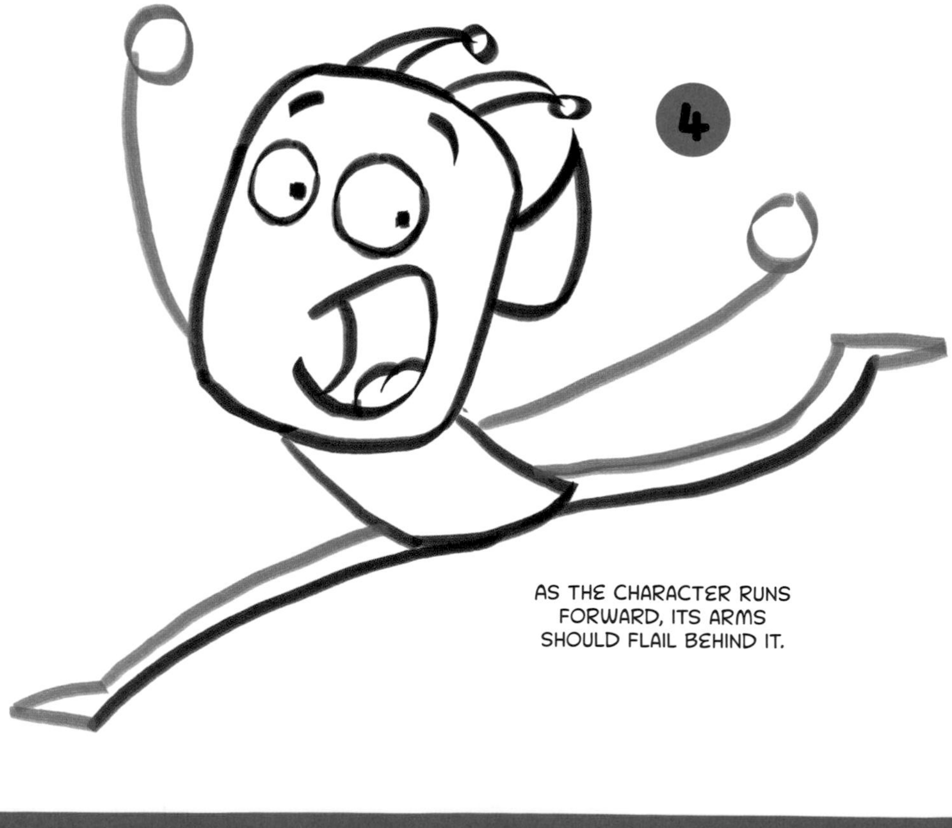

AS THE CHARACTER RUNS FORWARD, ITS ARMS SHOULD FLAIL BEHIND IT.

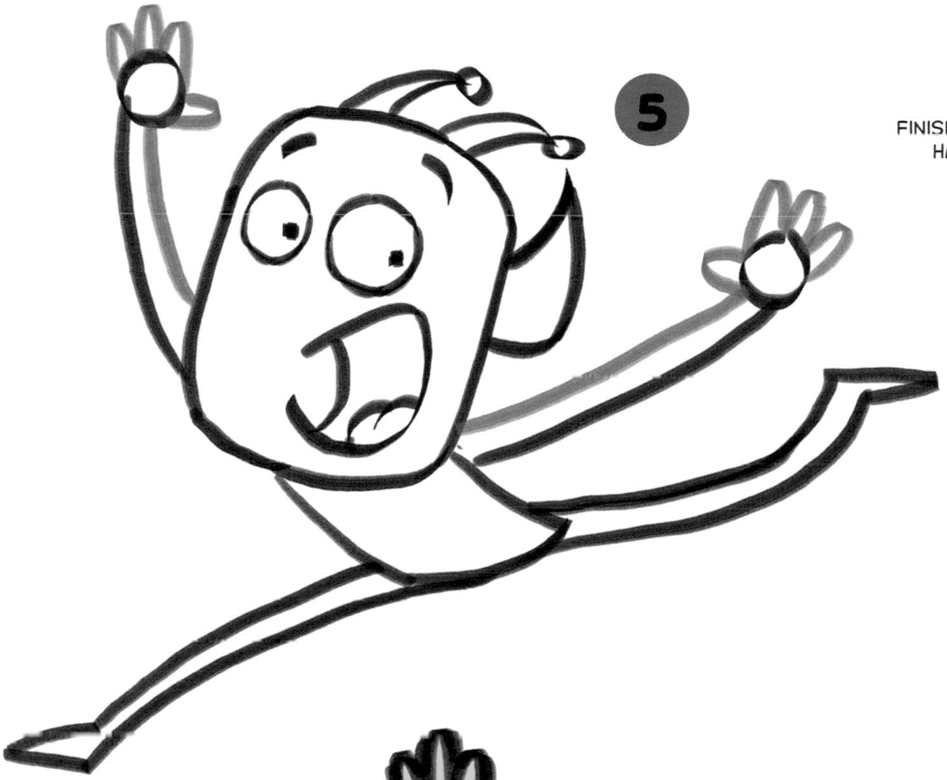

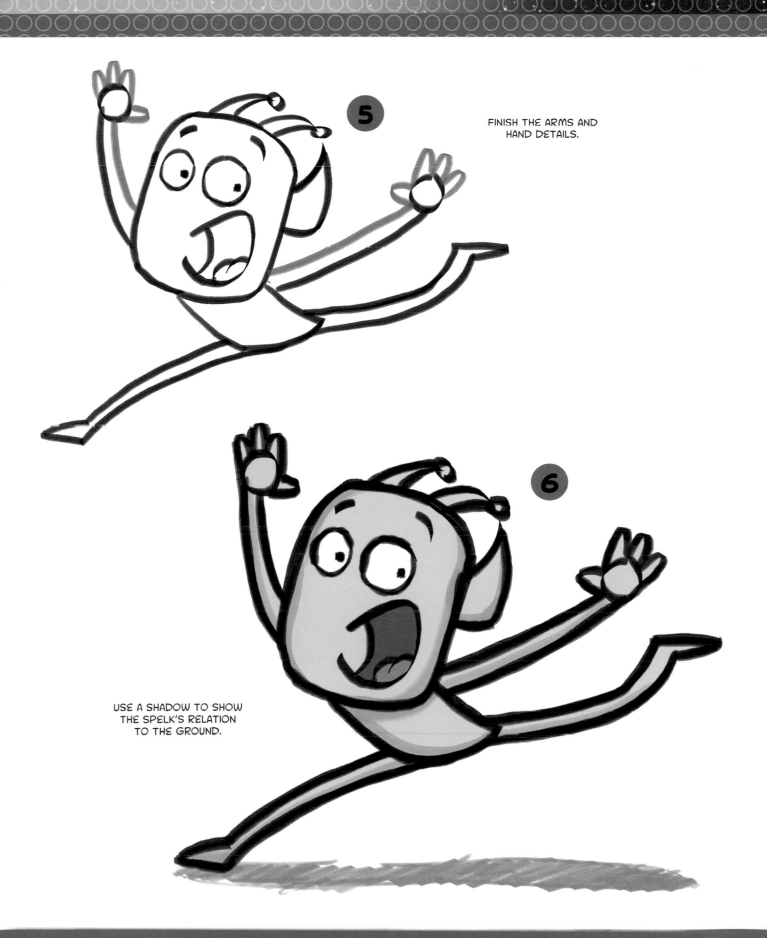

5

FINISH THE ARMS AND
HAND DETAILS.

6

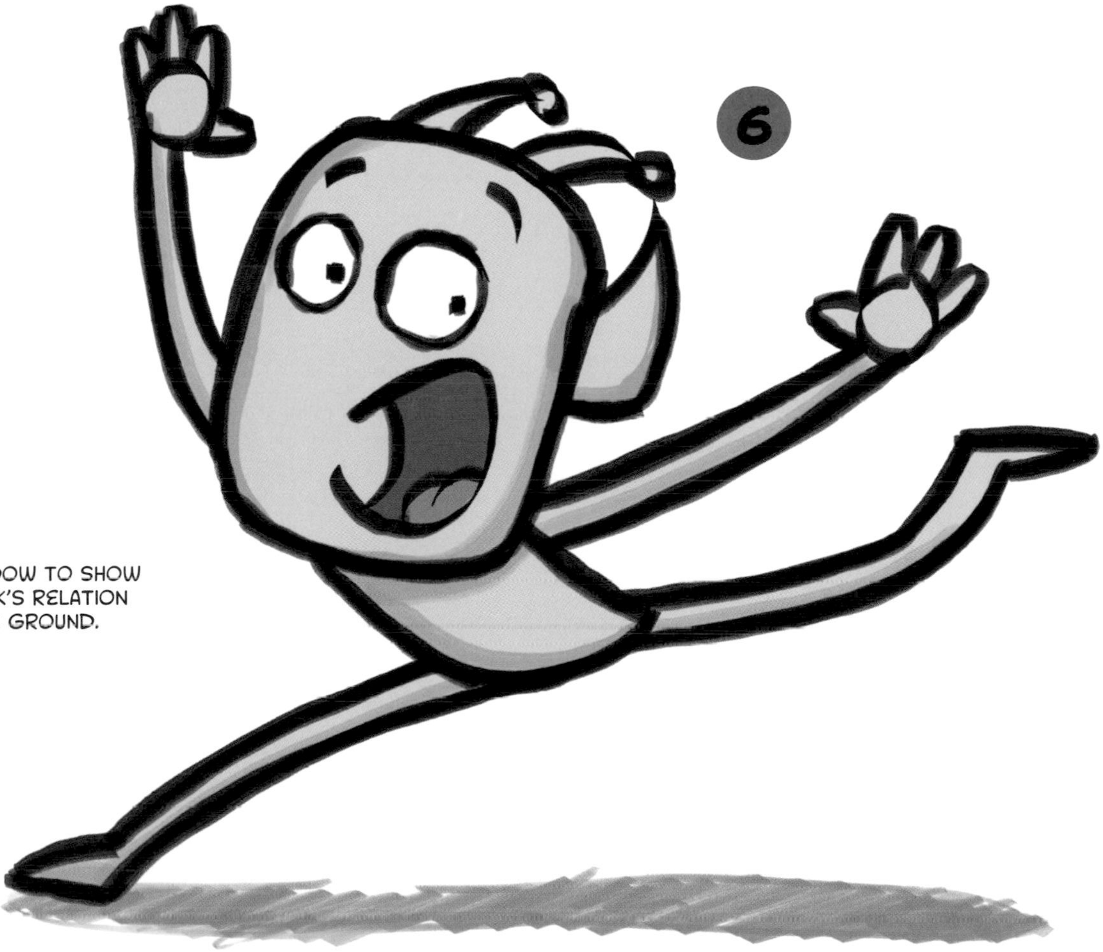

USE A SHADOW TO SHOW
THE SPELK'S RELATION
TO THE GROUND.

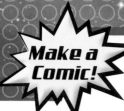

Adding Dialog

Now that your thumbnail sketches are complete and your panels laid out, add the dialog! Dialog boxes and balloons show conversations between characters, thoughts, shouts, whispers, sound effects, and narration about the scene or situation that the character is in.

Conversations

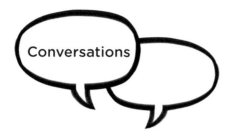

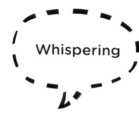

A NORMAL CONVERSATION HAS A SOLID SPEECH BALLOON.

Thoughts

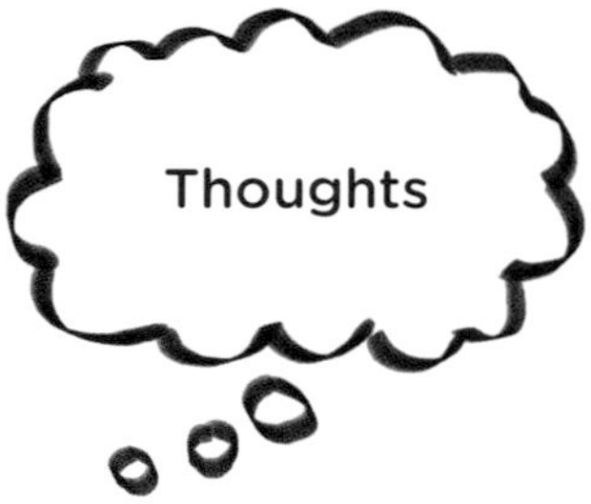

THOUGHT BALLOONS HAVE SOFTER EDGES LIKE A CLOUD.

Shouting

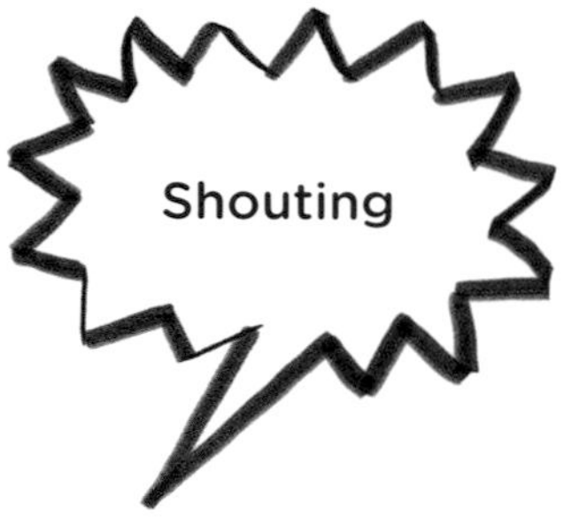

A SHOUTING DIALOG BOX HAS SHARP, JAGGED EDGES.

Whispering

A WHISPER IS DASHED LIKE IT'S BARELY EVEN THERE.

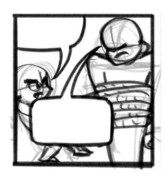

Carefully map out your dialog so the text won't distract from the action and overcrowd the page. The words and the art should work together to tell the story. A dialog box is covering up the action in the scene to the left. This obscures the reader's view; they aren't able to clearly see what's happening in the panel.

In English we read from top to bottom and across the page from left to right. Most readers scan over a page to look at the art and then go back to read the words. A strong panel at the top provides a good anchor for the whole page and entices people to keep reading.

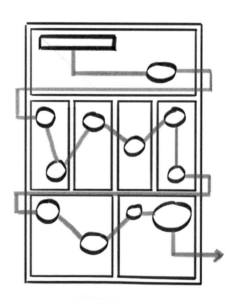

PUT NARRATION TEXT IN AN ENCLOSED RECTANGLE.

ILLUSTRATE SOUNDS LIKE "BLAM," "HISS," "POW," AND "ZAP."

PLACE DIALOG AWAY FROM THE MAIN ACTION, AND CLEARLY CONNECT THE TAILS OF THE BALLOONS TO THE SPEAKER IN EACH PANEL.

AVOID COVERING A FIGURE WITH THE DIALOG BOXES, BUT IF YOU MUST, DON'T COVER THEIR FACES.

DIALOG USUALLY LOOKS BEST AT THE TOP OF THE PANEL, AND, AS A GENERAL RULE, PLACE NO MORE THAN THREE SPEECH BALLOONS IN EACH PANEL.

Commander Cordy

Backstory: Cordy Seacliff is a child genius, and a little socially awkward. He loves to watch old sci-fi movies and is determined to bring their vision of the future into reality. That's why he created his own jetpack.
Motivation: Cordy sees the world in black and white, just like the movies he loves. He's out to be the noble hero.
Powers: He is a tech genius.
Limitations: Cordy is young and has had little experience with the world. While this can be a positive trait, in Cordy's case it has made him far too trusting of others.

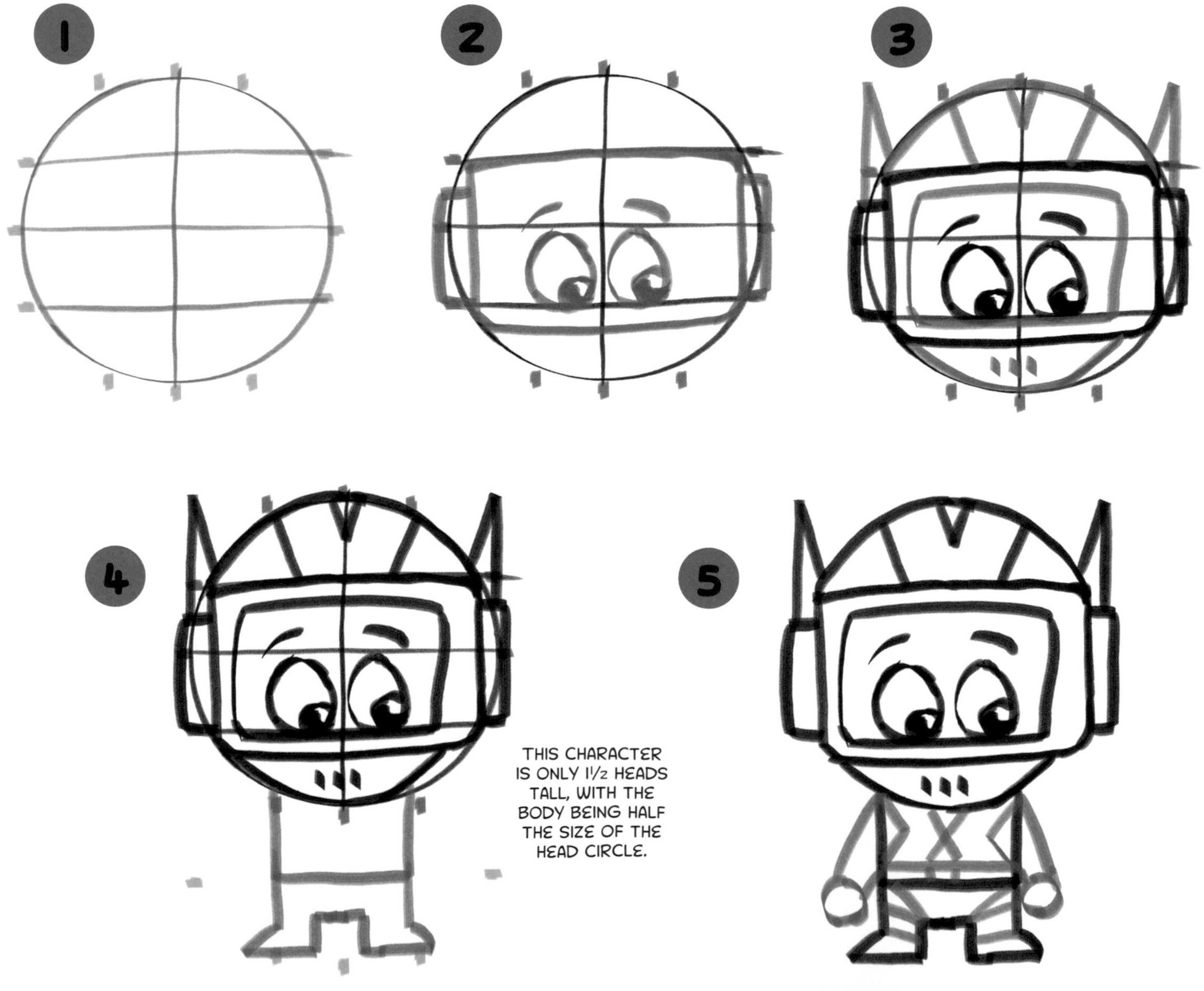
1
2
3
4
5
THIS CHARACTER IS ONLY 1½ HEADS TALL, WITH THE BODY BEING HALF THE SIZE OF THE HEAD CIRCLE.

6

START WITH A SIMPLE BOX FOR THE JETPACK AND THEN ADD THE EXTRA DETAILS TO FILL IT OUT.

7

8

S.A.V.A.G.E.

Backstory: Masked wrestler Santo Argozan Verdanto Abismo Guerrero Eigeno adopted the names of the greatest luchadores of all time in an attempt to be listed among them. With his mystic Lagartija mask, he was transformed into The S.A.V.A.G.E.

Motivation: The S.A.V.A.G.E. has become obsessed with being the best of the best.

Powers: The S.A.V.A.G.E. has many reptilian powers, including wall-climbing, speed, leaping, and of course, tail regeneration.

Limitations: His vanity can get the best of him. The S.A.V.A.G.E. seems to be unable to refuse any challenge that could result in his increased status and reputation.

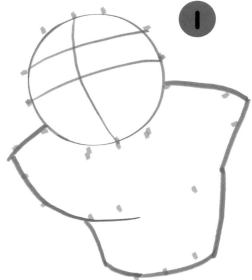

1

THE HEIGHT OF THE HEAD CIRCLE AND TORSO ARE THE SAME.

2

DRAW THE MOUTH AND EYES ON THE HORIZONTAL GUIDELINES. THE LEGS ARE HALF AS TALL AS THE HEAD CIRCLE.

3

SKETCH IN THE OUTLINE OF THE ARMS AND ERASE THE GUIDELINES.

4

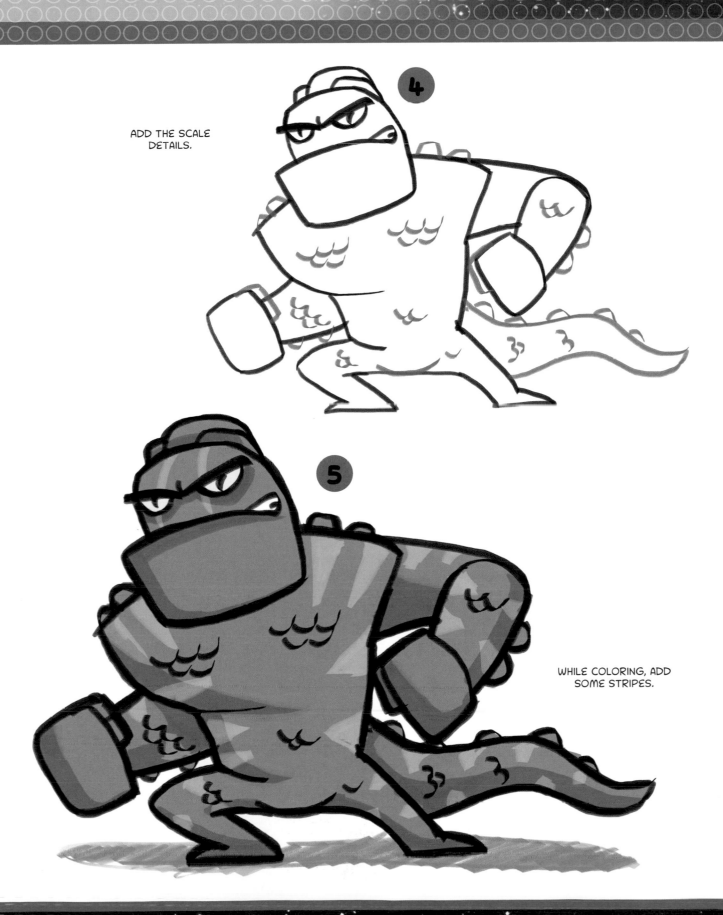

ADD THE SCALE DETAILS.

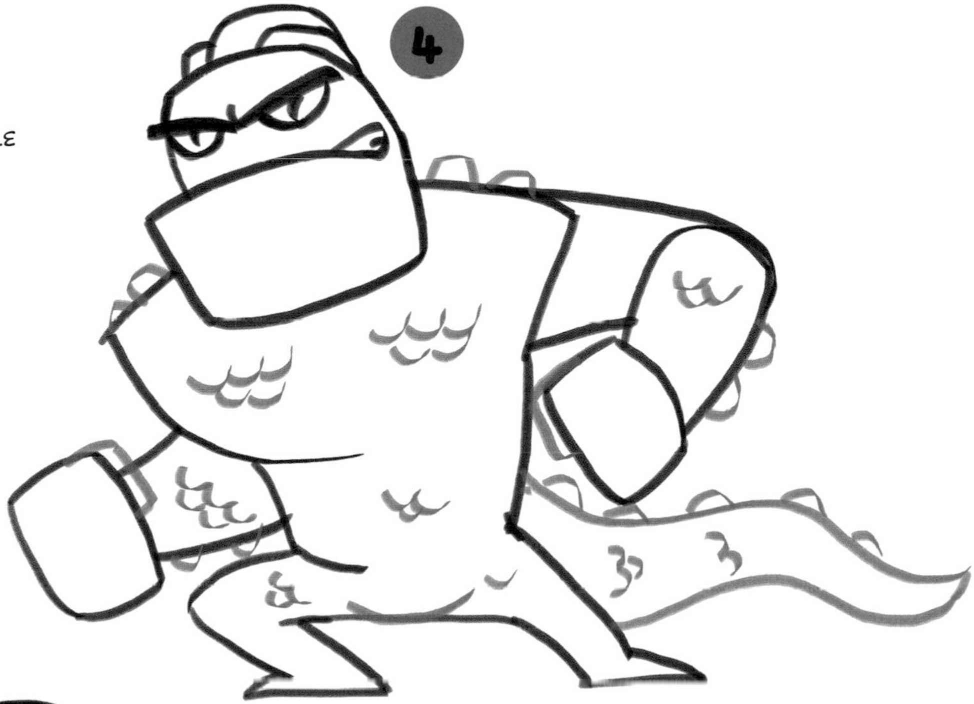

5

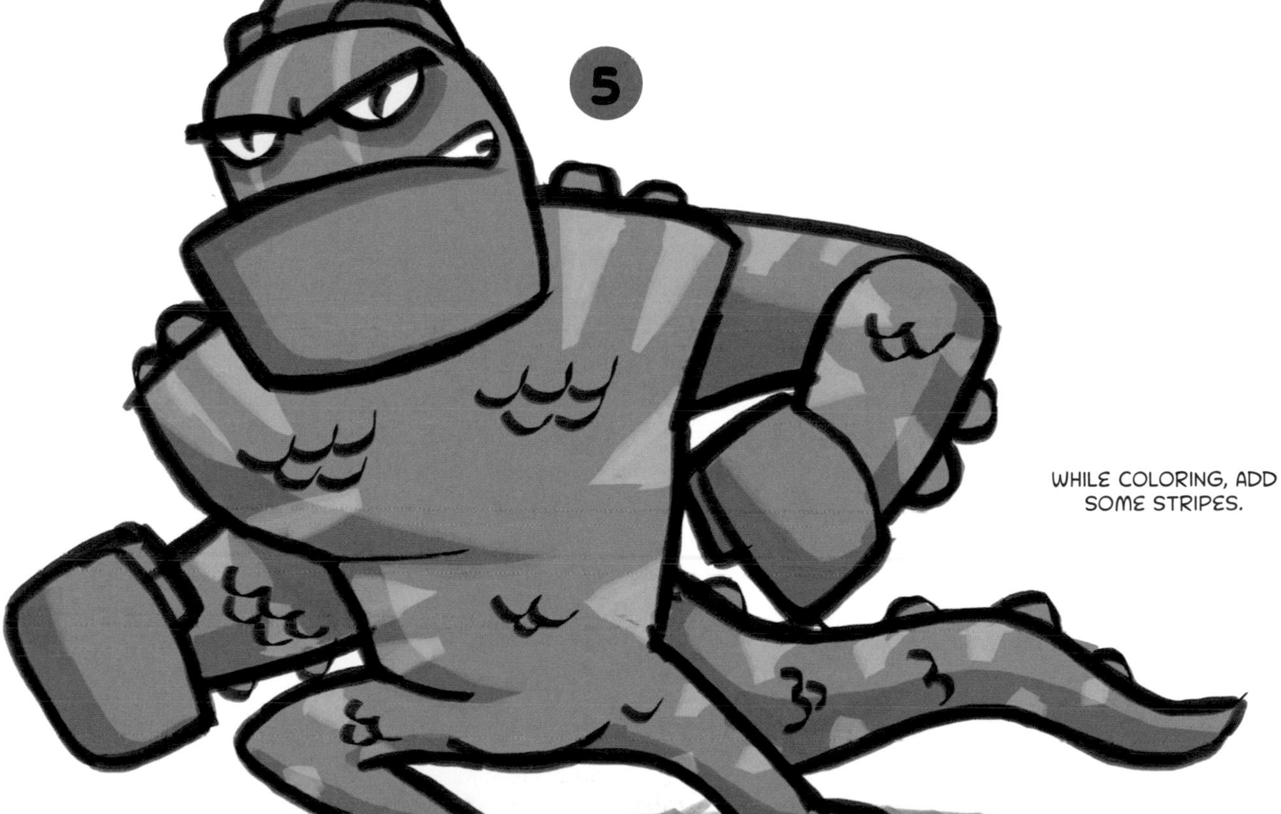

WHILE COLORING, ADD SOME STRIPES.

Babsti

Backstory: Professor Kylie Cattsen is an expert Egyptologist. During an excavation, she fell through a trapdoor and discovered the secrets of the ancient City of Bubastis, sacred to the Egyptian cat goddess Bastet.

Motivation: Babsti wants to re-establish the rule of cats and create a new City of Bubastis.

Powers: She is agile, sneaky, and always lands on her feet. While it has yet to be tested, it is rumored that through the power of Bubastis, Babsti has nine lives.

Limitations: She has a weakness for yarn balls and laser pointers.

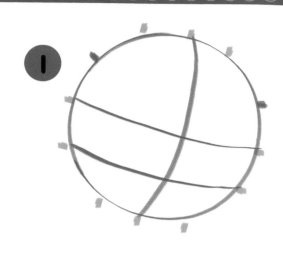

1

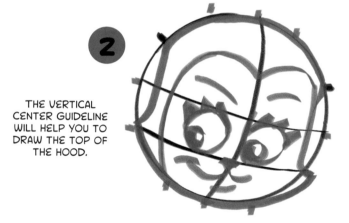

2

THE VERTICAL CENTER GUIDELINE WILL HELP YOU TO DRAW THE TOP OF THE HOOD.

3

THE EARS FOR THIS CHARACTER DO NOT LINE UP WITH THE EYES.

4

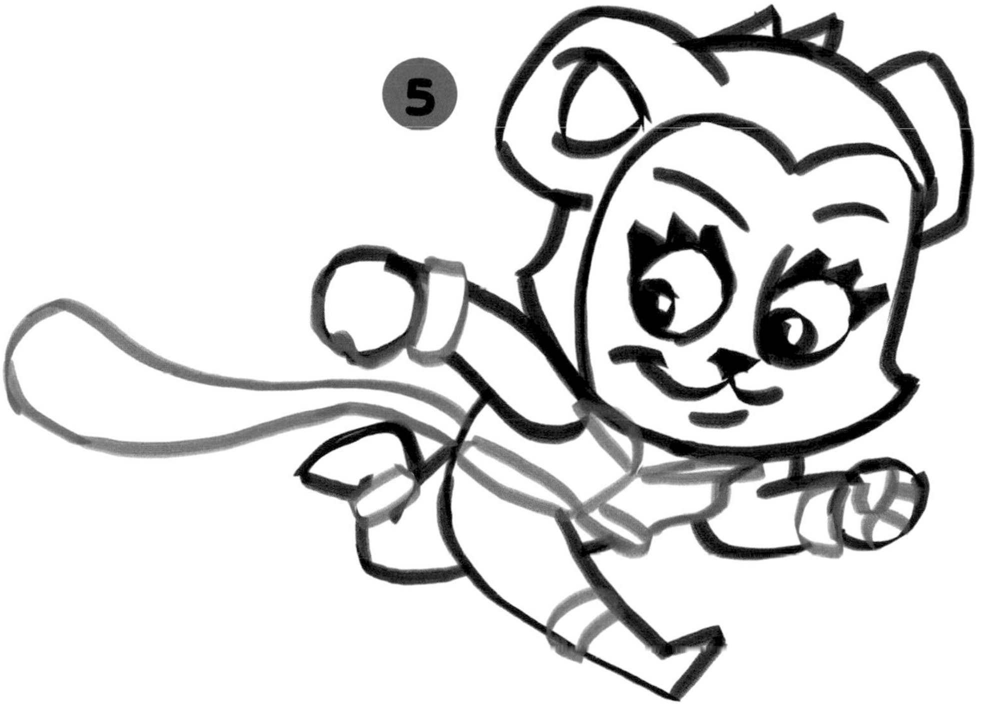

DRAW THE TAIL FLOWING OUT BEHIND TO ADD MORE DYNAMIC ACTION TO THE POSE.

ADD STRIPES TO BABSTI'S COSTUME DURING THE COLORING STAGE.

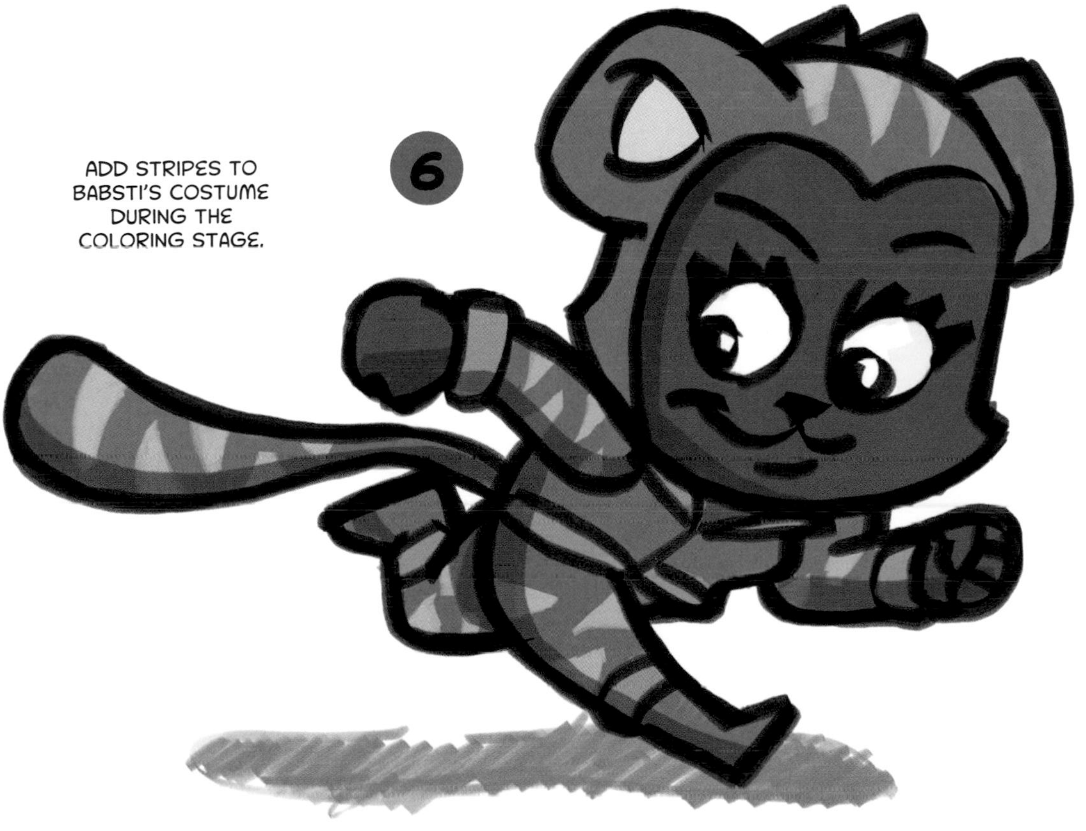

Backstory: Riela is one of the elite guards entrusted with the protection of the royal family. The underwater kingdom of Valence is in turmoil due to the disappearance of the prince. Riela had been sent on a quest to find the lost prince.

Motivation: As a royal guard, Riela feels personally responsible for the missing prince.

Powers: Riela can breathe in water and on land and has the ability to shift her appearance from a tail to legs. She can control the water, as well as the moisture in the air.

Limitations: She must avoid heat and dehydration at all costs.

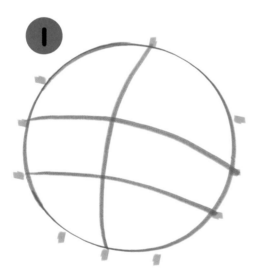

EVEN THE MOST COMPLICATED DRAWING WILL START WITH A SIMPLE SHAPE, LIKE THIS CIRCLE.

THE EYES AND EARS ARE ALIGNED, JUST LIKE ON MANY OF THE PREVIOUS CHARACTERS.

3

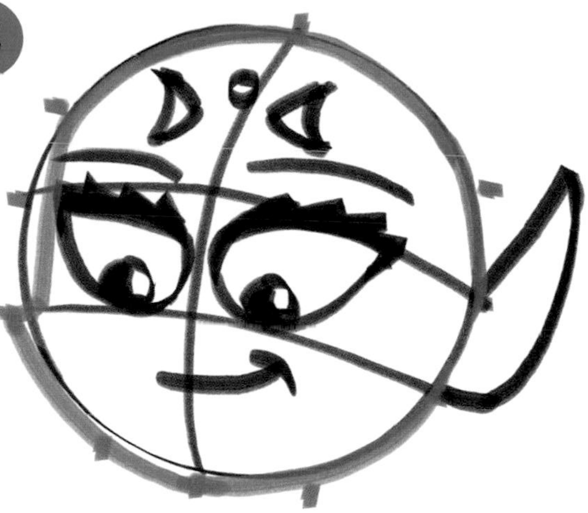

MARK THE HEIGHT OF THE BODY, WHICH IS THE SAME AS THE HEIGHT OF THE HEAD CIRCLE. DRAW A BOX SHAPE ENDING HALFWAY DOWN THE BODY.

4

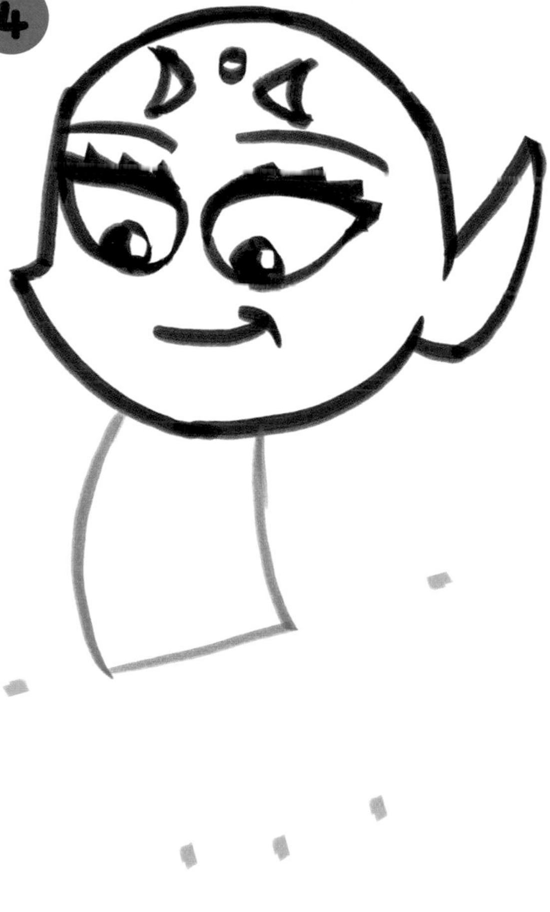

5

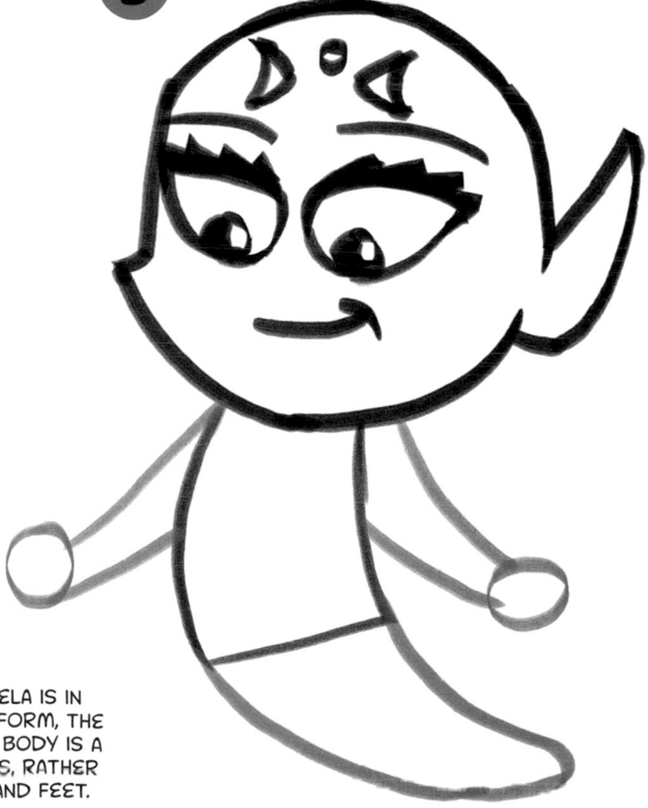

BECAUSE RIELA IS IN HER AQUATIC FORM, THE REST OF HER BODY IS A TAIL WITH FINS, RATHER THAN LEGS AND FEET.

6

ADD THE SCALE DETAILS TO THE TAIL AS WELL AS THE FINS AND SHIRT.

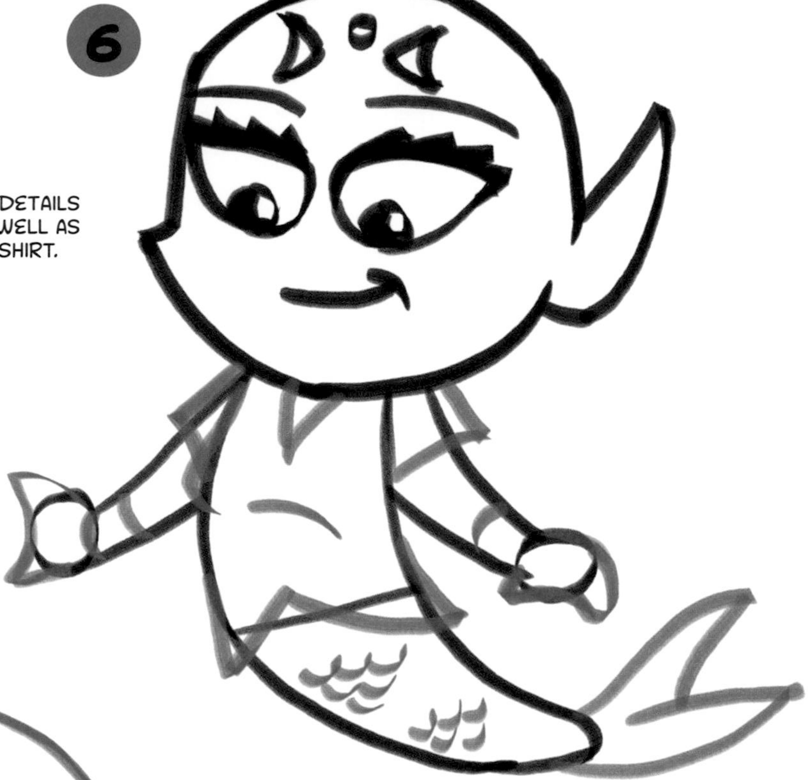

7

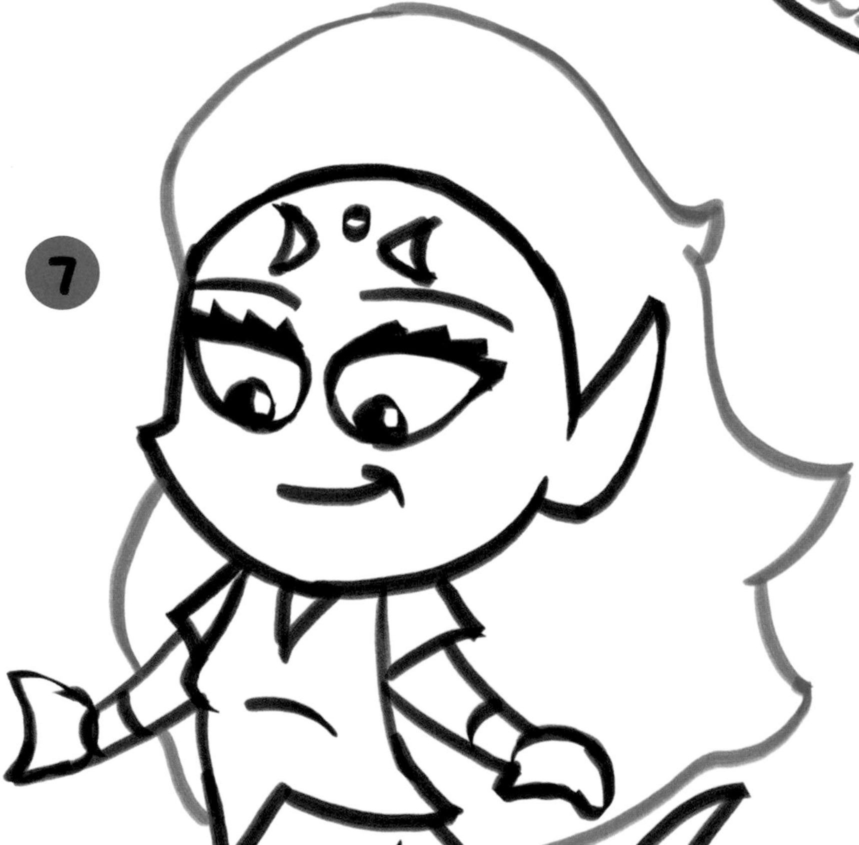

RIELA HAS REALLY BIG HAIR, SO IT'S BEST TO WAIT UNTIL THE END TO MAKE SURE IT ALL FITS.

THE SHAPE OF RIELA'S EYES AND EARS,
AS WELL AS THE COLORING SEEMS
FAMILIAR... COULD THIS BE A CLUE
LEADING TO THE MISSING PRINCE?

The Vortexer

Backstory: Tim Tanner's roommate mistook his science experiment for a hot pepper and ate it. This resulted in his roommate becoming the hero "Kaoh," but Tim was never recognized for the part he played in creating a hero. Tim used his scientific abilities to become Kaoh's nemesis, The Vortexer.
Motivation: Tim wants nothing more than to defeat Kaoh and to show the world that he deserves all the credit.

BECAUSE THIS CHARACTER IS LOOKING DOWNWARD, DRAW THE HORIZONTAL AND VERTICAL GUIDELINES ACCORDINGLY.

1

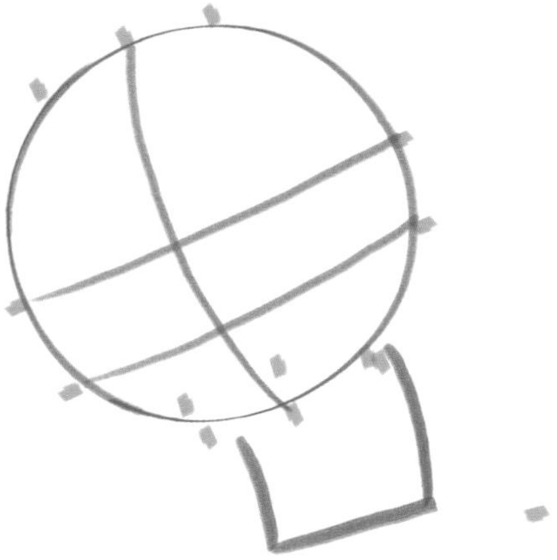

2

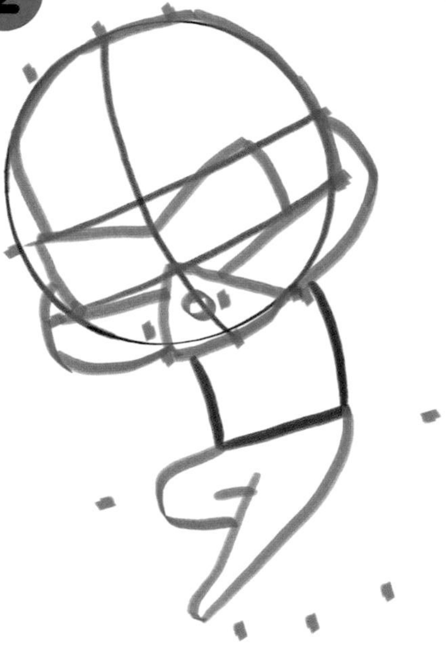

3

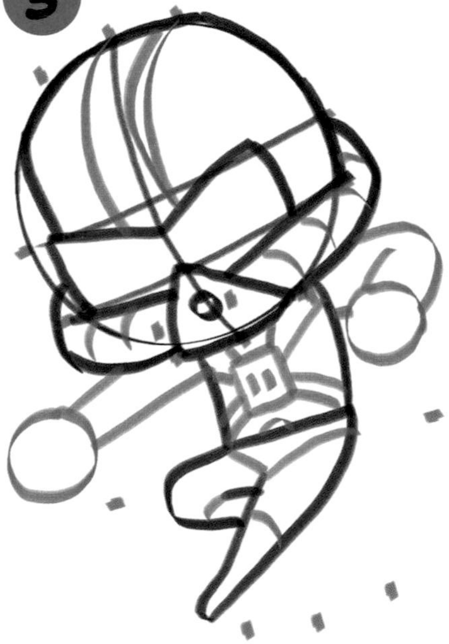

ADD THE COSTUME AND HELMET DETAILS.

4

TO CREATE THE VORTEX EFFECT, DRAW A SERIES OF LIGHT CIRCLES THAT INCREASE IN SIZE FROM RIGHT TO LEFT.

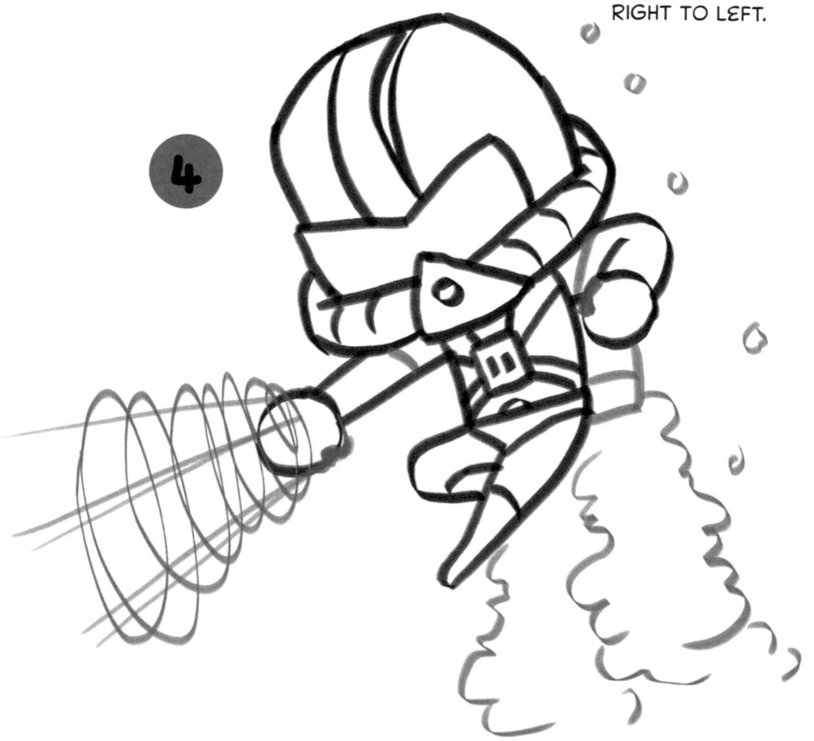

Powers: He wears a technologically enhanced, fire-resistant super suit with wrist-mounted, fire-suppressant vortex cannons.

Limitations: Tim's a genius in a lot of ways, but he hasn't figured out how to make his batteries last longer.

ADD SOME GRAY TO THE VORTEX AS WELL AS THE EXHAUST FROM THE VORTEXER'S JETPACK, BUT LEAVE MUCH OF IT WHITE.

Make It Your Own!

Now make changes to Babsti (page 78) and The Vortexer (page 84) to create totally new characters. What do you think these characters' names should be? What are their backstories and motivations, their powers and limitations?

1

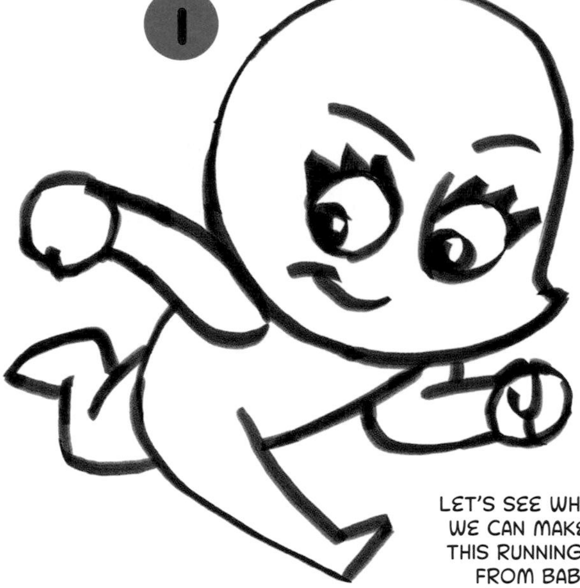

LET'S SEE WHO ELSE WE CAN MAKE WITH THIS RUNNING POSE FROM BABSTI!

2

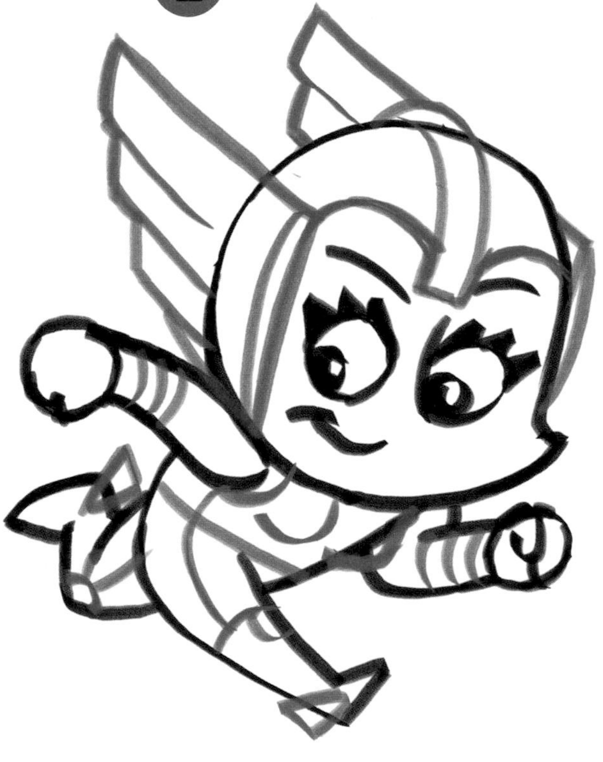

BECAUSE THIS CHARACTER IS RUNNING, LET'S GIVE HER A WINGED HELMET AND SOME METALLIC FLYING SHOES.

3

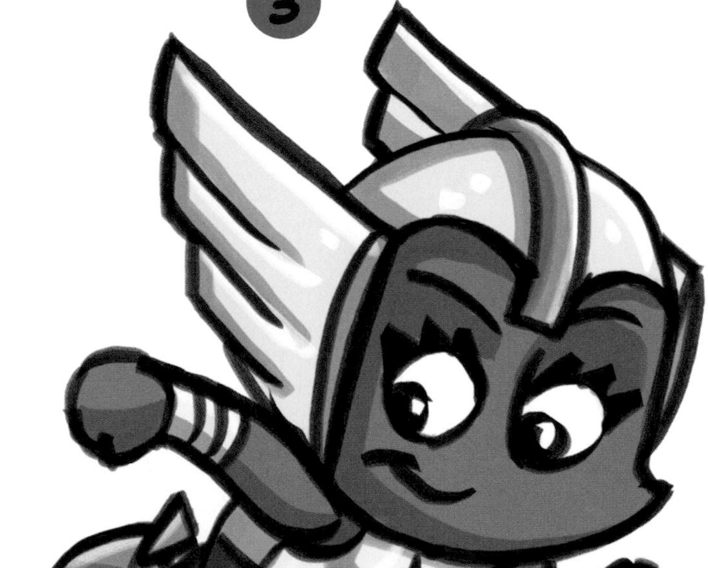

1

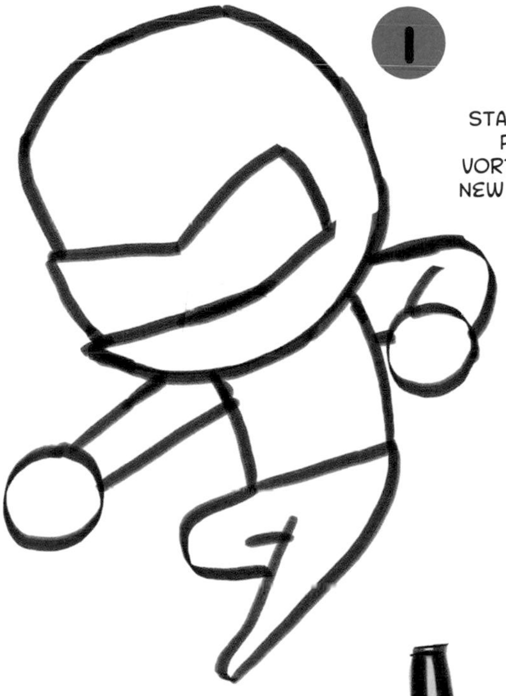

START WITH THE BASIC POSE FROM THE VORTEXER TO DESIGN A NEW FLYING CHARACTER.

2

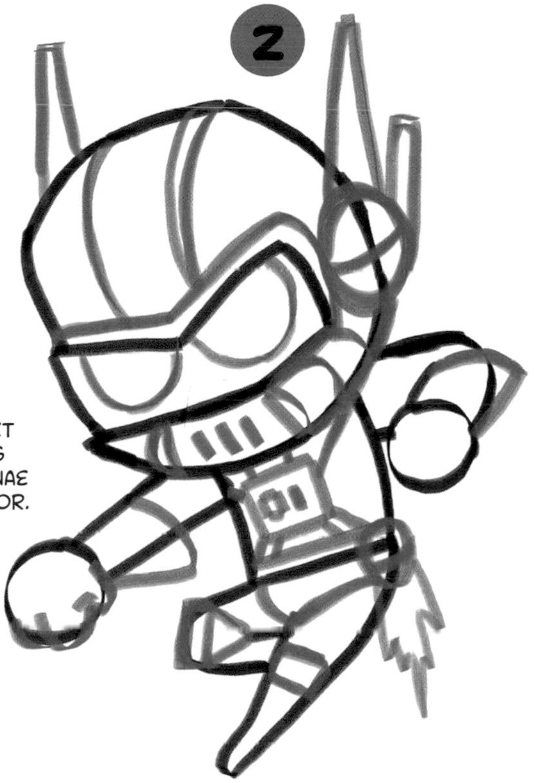

MODIFY THE HELMET DESIGN BY ADDING SOME EXTRA ANTENNAE AND EYES IN THE VISOR.

3

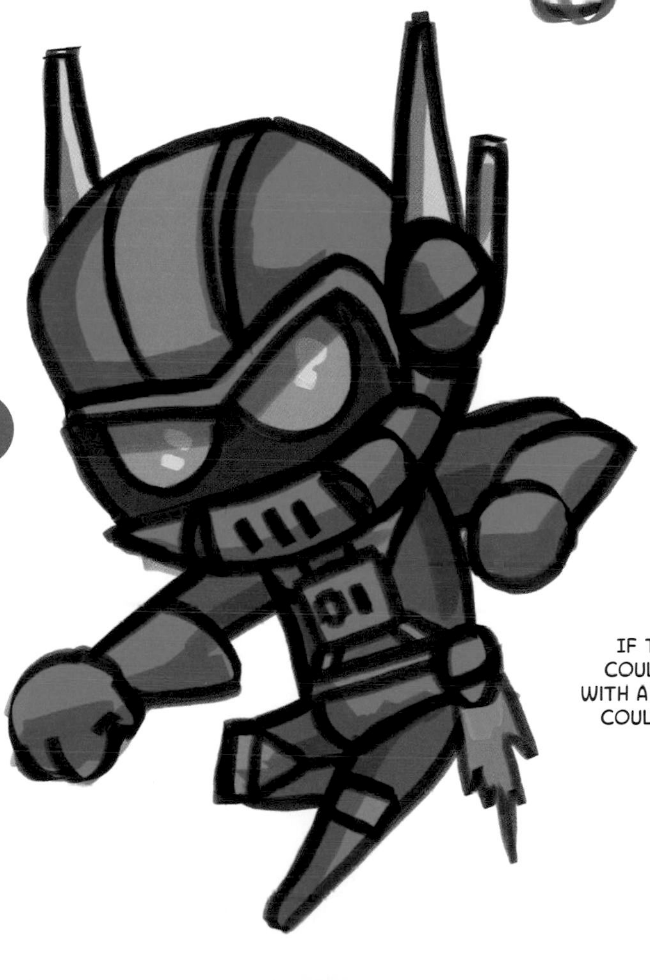

IF THIS NEW CHARACTER COULD FREEZE MACHINERY WITH A SINGLE BLAST, HIS NAME COULD BE RUSS T. WALKER!

Putting It All Together

Comic books are a visual form of storytelling. The pictures and words on each page are divided into panels to create action, drama, pacing, and an overall tone for the story. There's a fine balance between the visuals and the written word, but the key to a successful comic is the story that's being told. Keep this in mind when you're putting all the elements together to create your comic book.

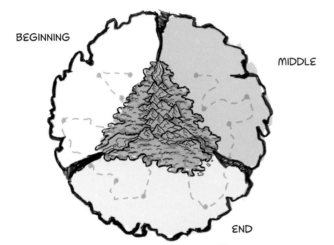

BEGINNING

MIDDLE

END

When starting your comic, first ask yourself, "How would I summarize my story?" Always keep this brief description in mind so your story will stay on track. Determine your story's beginning, middle, and end.

Then look at your characters in detail. What are their backstories, their motivations, their powers, and their weaknesses? How do they deal with the conflict they must overcome on their journey?

  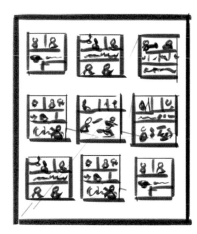

Before you write a single line of dialog, sketch out the story elements. From this rough outline, write the script and refine and improve your thumbnail sketches. Divide the pages into panels, and map out the dialog boxes and speech balloons. Now that it's all pulled together, finalize all the drawings and text, and you have a complete comic book!

The process of making a comic can be lengthy, but remember, not every panel has to be a fully formed masterpiece. Work in a way that best suits your style, keep your goals in mind, and don't give up!

Standing Characters

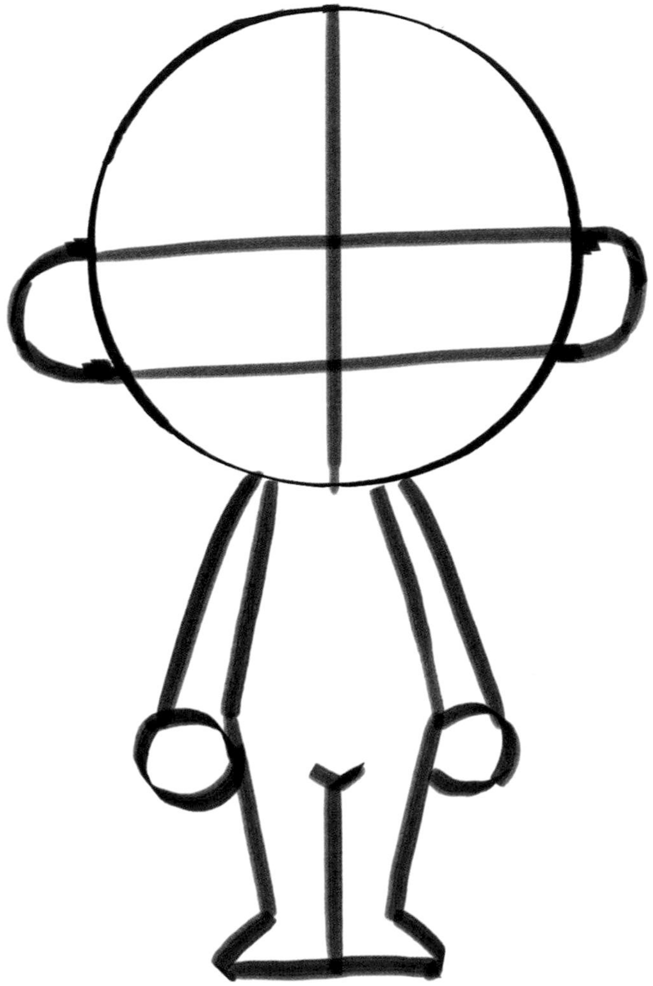

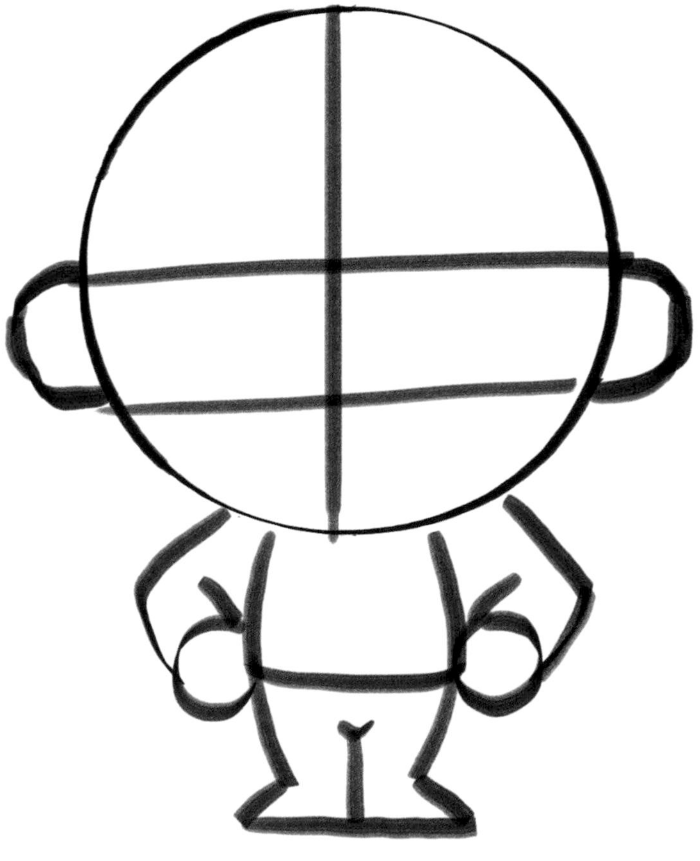

Alien Characters

Flying Characters

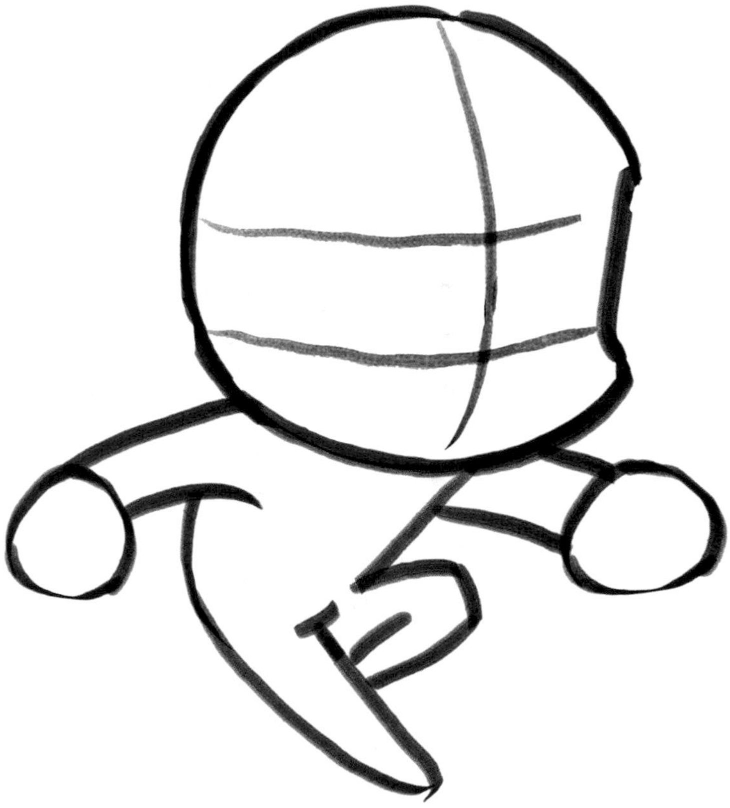

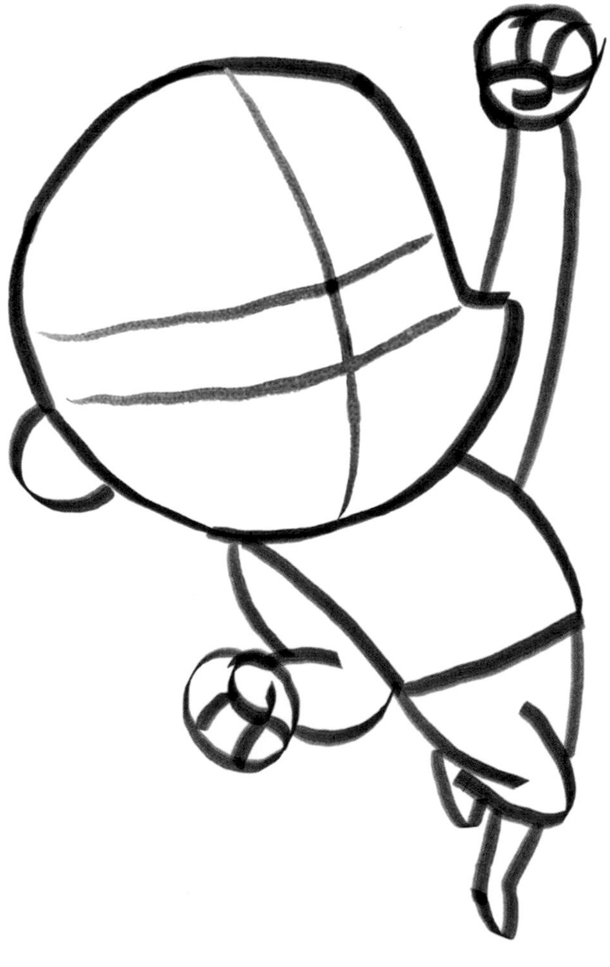

Fighting Characters

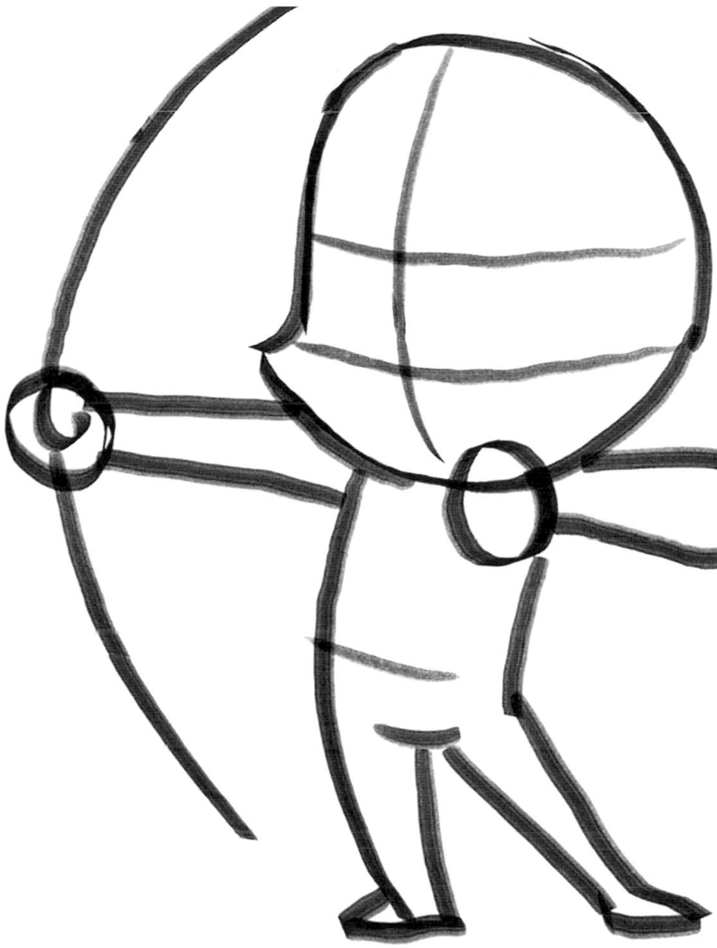

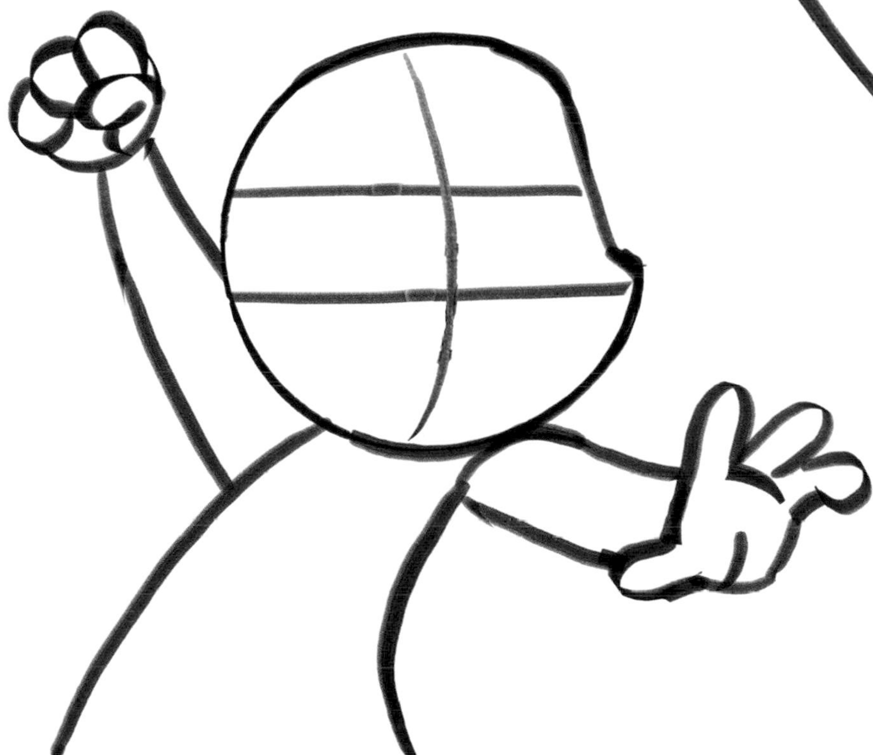

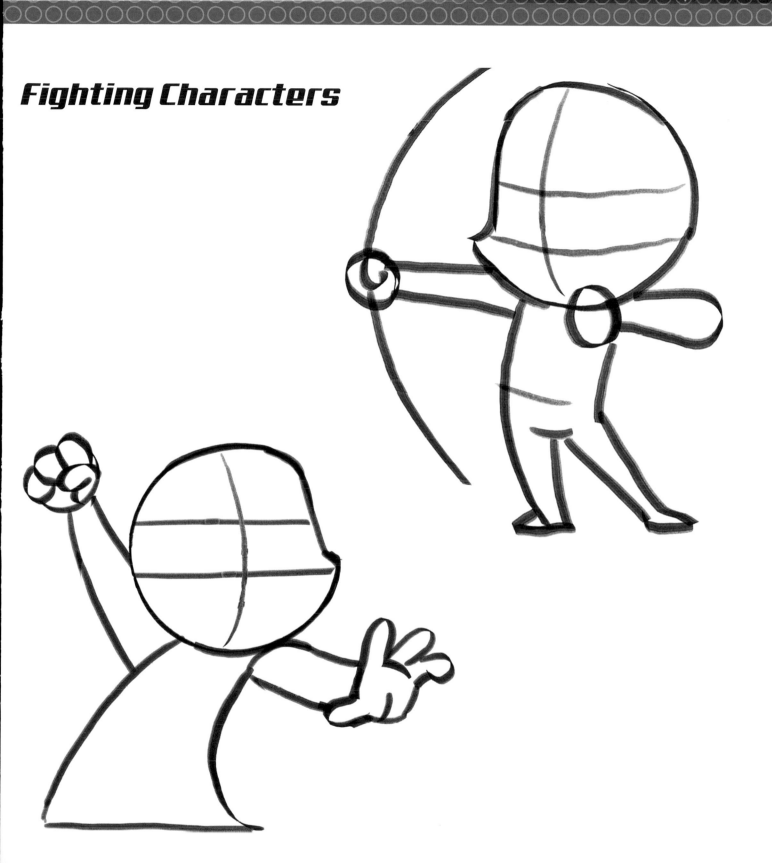

Characters in Action

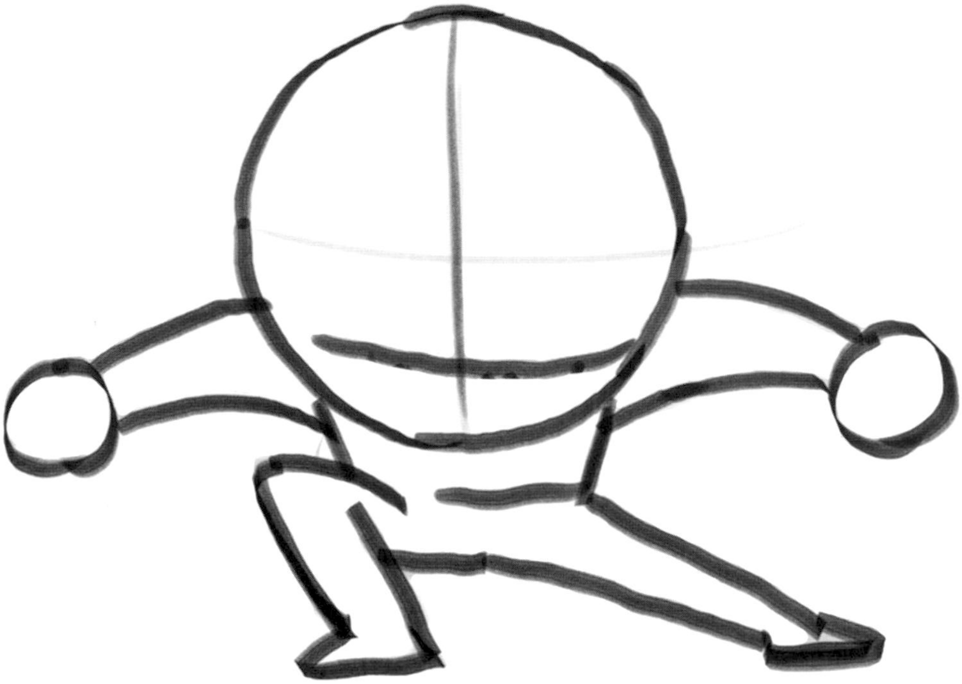

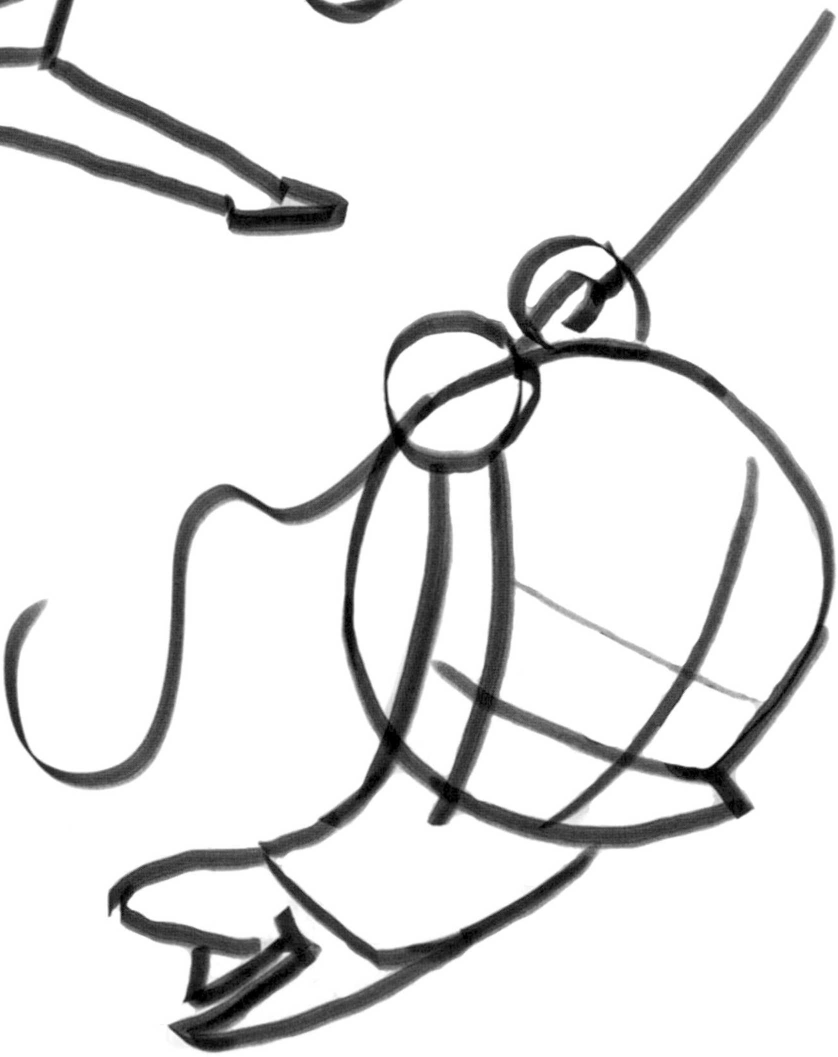

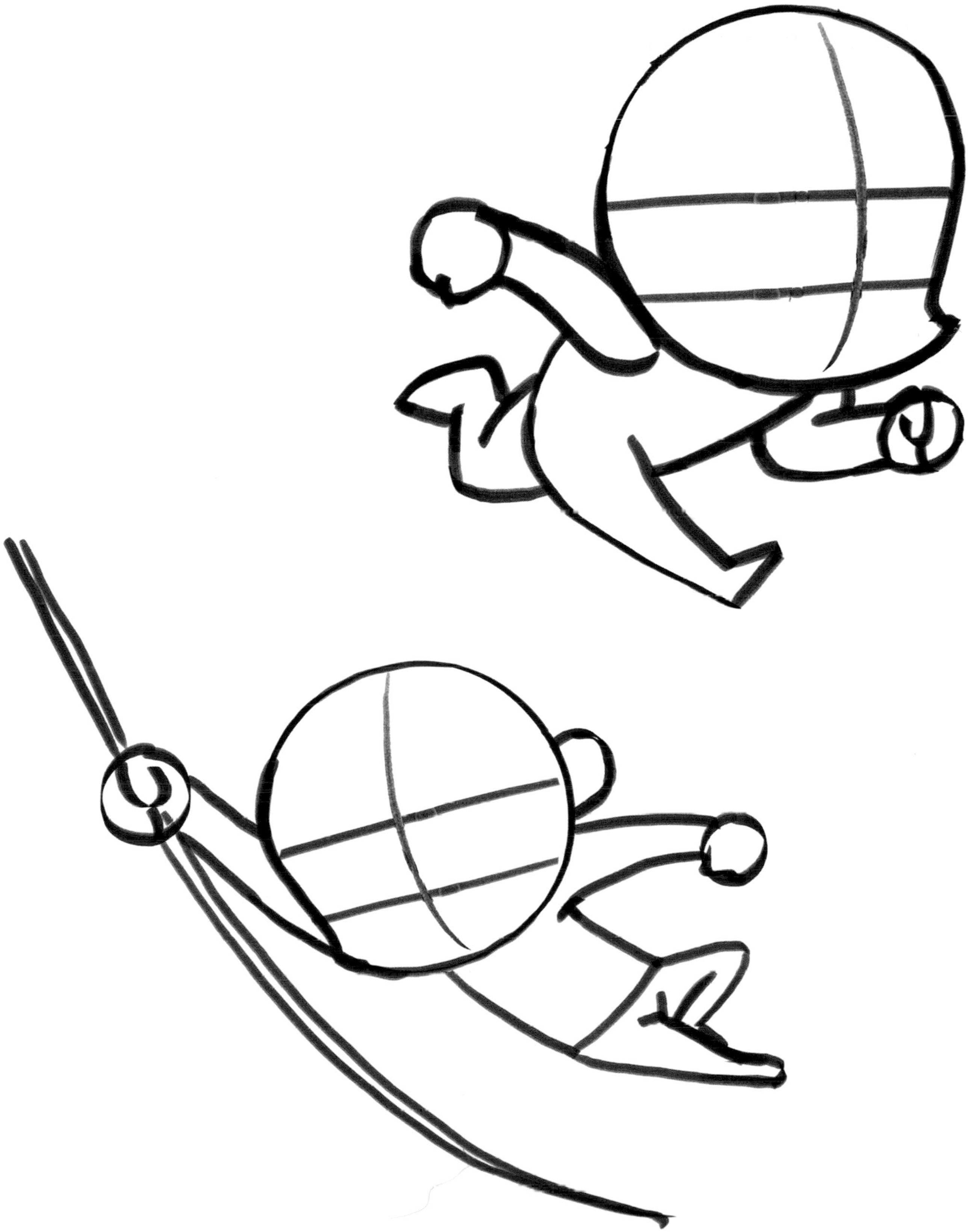

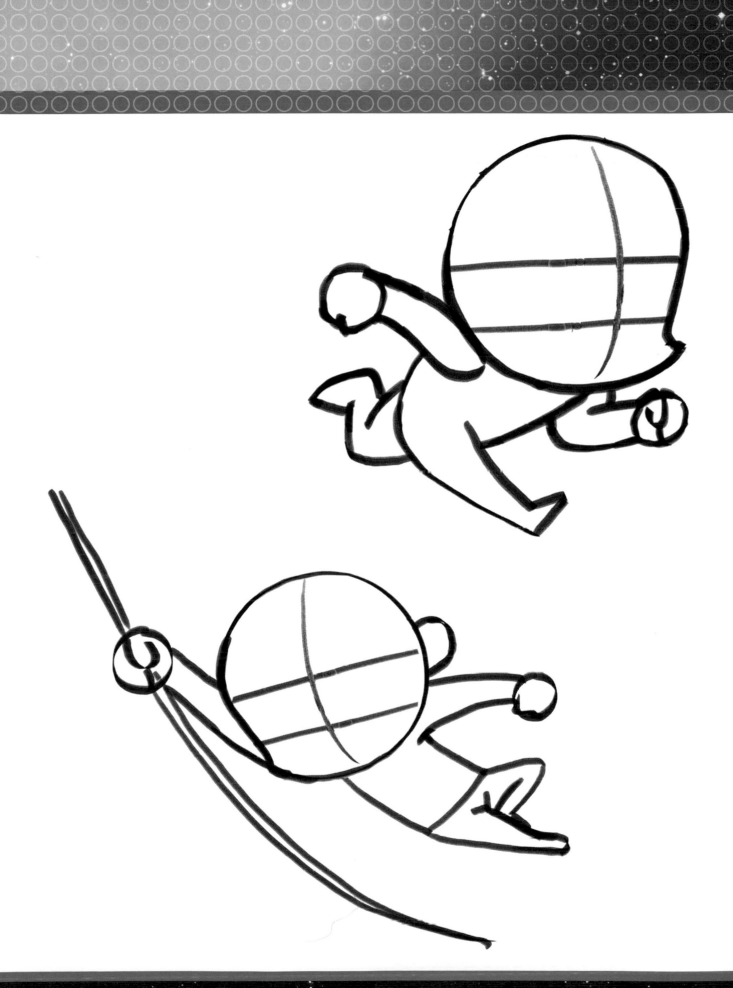

About the Author

Spencer Brinkerhoff III started drawing and making art at an early age and has never stopped, completing a fine arts degree at Arizona State University and establishing a career as an artist. Spencer's professional work has included creating some of the horse sculptures for P.F. Chang's restaurants, animating an educational game for the World Health Organization, creating and starring in a video that won him Burt Reynolds' Trans Am, and creating *Star Wars* art for Lucasfilm Ltd. In addition to working on these licensed projects, he has also created a glasses-less 3-D image platform called ShadowBox Comics, an in-camera special effect key chain called LightStickFX, and a drawing system called DrawingIsSimple. Spencer lives in the greater Phoenix area of Arizona. Visit his website www.drawingissimple.com and find him on social media @spencerb3 for more!